점프 업
파닉스 **Jump Up**
Phonics **4**
개정판

점프 업 파닉스 4 [개정판]

2008년 05월 20일 초판 1쇄 발행
2025년 04월 15일 개정 1쇄 발행

지은이 문호준/국제어학연구소 영어학부
그림 이경택
펴낸이 이규인
펴낸곳 국제어학연구소 출판부
출판등록 2010년 1월 18일 제302-2010-000006호
주소 서울특별시 마포구 대흥로4길 49, 1층(용강동 월명빌딩)
Tel (02) 704-0900 **팩시밀리** (02) 703-5117
홈페이지 www.bookcamp.co.kr
e-mail changbook1@hanmail.net
ISBN 979-11-9880105-0 13740
정가 18,000원

점프 업 파닉스

Jump Up Phonics 4 개정판

글 문호준·국제어학연구소 영어학부

ILR 국제어학연구소

CONTENTS

There are a man and a sheep
under the tree.
It's time for lunch.
The man eats meat and drinks tea.
The sheep eats a big leaf and beans.
A bee wants to eat, too.
The man and the sheep
feed the bee.

Sounds

Listen and repeat.

1.  **b**   **ee** _____
2.  **tr**   **ee** _____
3.  **s**   **ea** _____
4. **t**   **ea** _____

Match and write.

1.  s •   • ee  _____ •

2.  t •   • ea  _____ •

3. 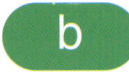 b •   • ee  _____ •

4.  tr •   • ea  _____ •

Listen, point and repeat.

b**ee**	f**ee**t	f**ee**d
sh**ee**p	sl**ee**p	tr**ee**
eat	s**ea**	b**ea**n
m**ea**t	l**ea**f	t**ea**

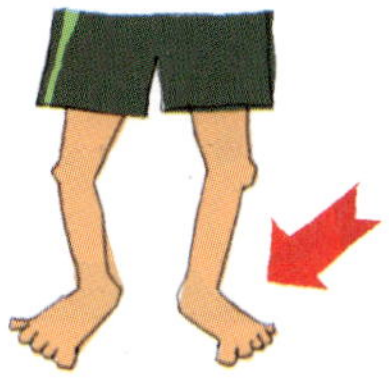

Sort and write the words according to the vowel sounds.

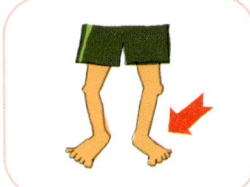   

ee

bee
feed

ea

sea tea

Listen, circle and write.

1

_____

2

_____

3

_____

4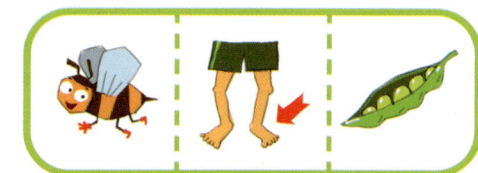

_____

5

_____

6

_____

7

_____

8

_____

Practice – Read

Read and find the correct sentence for the picture.

(a)

(b)

(c)

(d)

(e)

(f)

1 The kid swims in the sea. ☐

2 The man sleeps under the tree. ☐

3 The bee drinks some tea. ☐

4 The kid feeds chicks. ☐

5 The sheep eats a leaf. ☐

6 The monster has three feet. ☐

Circle the correct letters and write the word.

1
b
ee | ea

_____

2
b
ee | ea
n

_____

3
t
ee | ea

_____

4
tr
ee | ea

_____

5
ee | ea
t

_____

6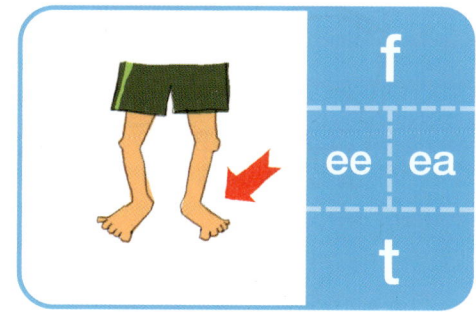
f
ee | ea
t

_____

Circle correct words and complete the story.

- There are a man and a  _____ under the tree.

- It's time for lunch.

- The man eats meat and drinks _____.

- The _____ eats a big _____ and beans.

- A _____ wants to eat, too.

- The man and the _____ feed the _____.

Activity *chant*

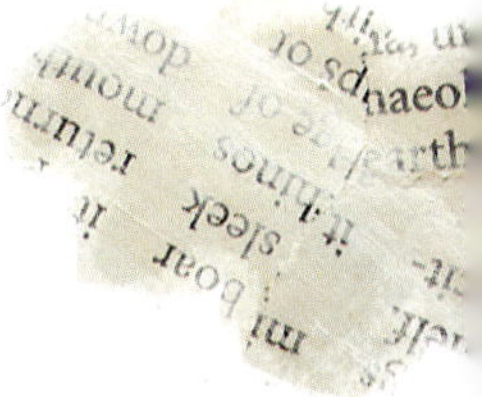

Whale whale, where are you?
I am in the sea.

Sheep sheep, where are you?
I am under the tree.

Bean bean, where are you?
I am on the meat.

Bees bees, where are you?
We are on your feet.

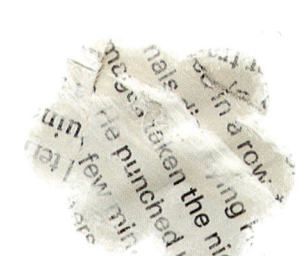

A dinosaur and a sheep
want to ride the seesaw.
They sit on the seesaw.
But the seesaw doesn't go up and down.
The dinosaur is big and heavy,
but the sheep is small and light.
The sheep brings her two more friends.
Now, they can play on the seesaw
and have fun.

Listen and repeat.

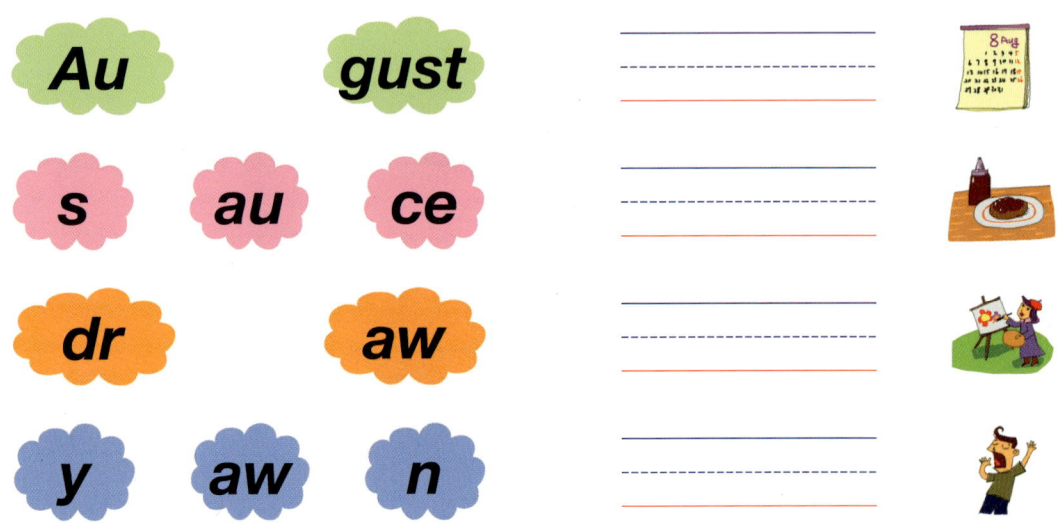

Au	**gust**	
s	**au**	**ce**
dr	**aw**	
y	**aw**	**n**

Match and write.

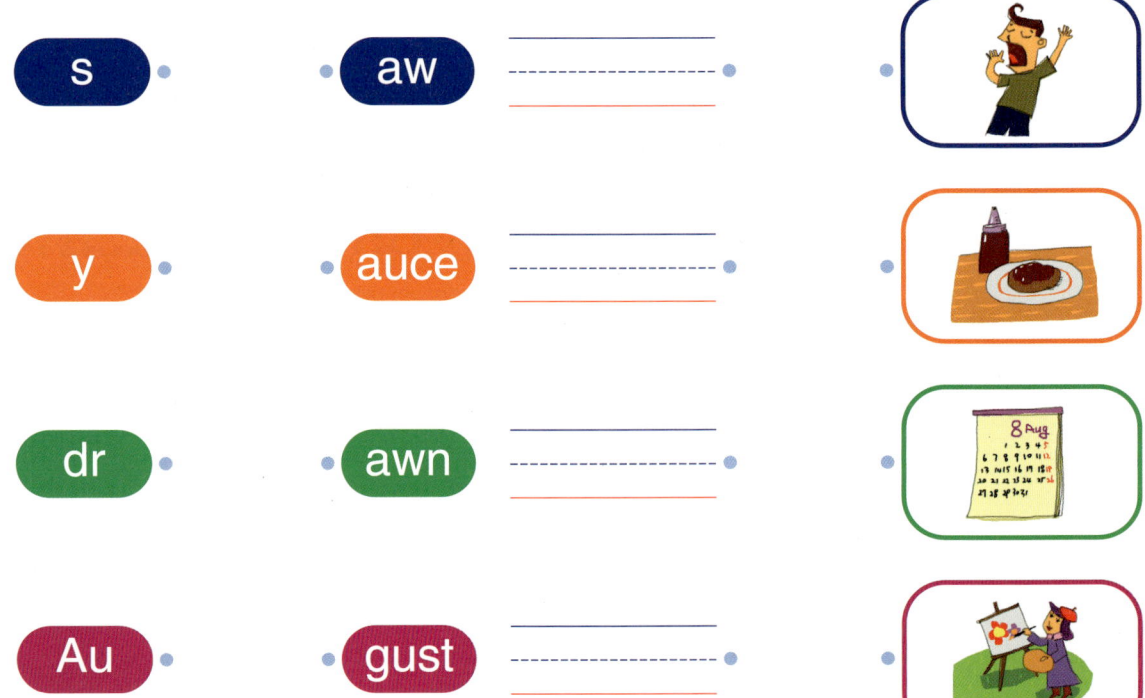

s	aw
y	auce
dr	awn
Au	gust

Double Letters au aw **_New words_**

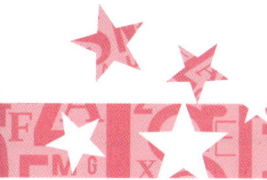

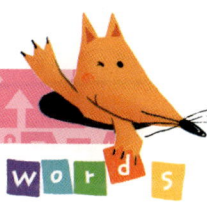

Listen, point and repeat.

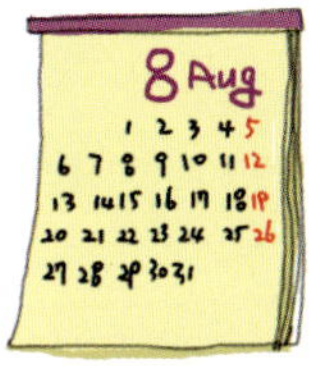

August

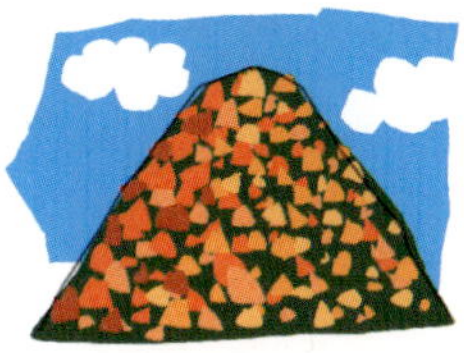

autumn

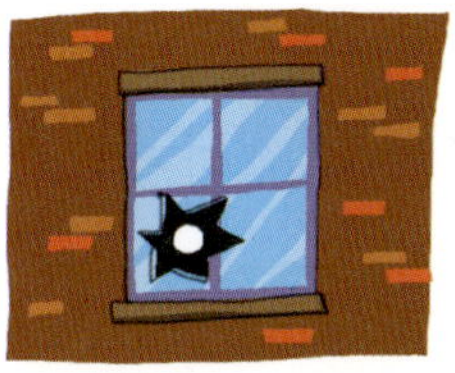

fault

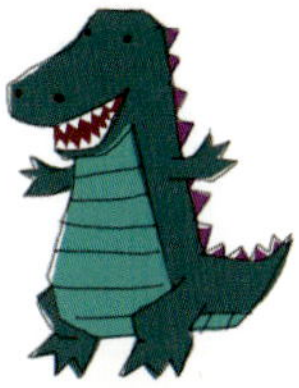

dinosaur

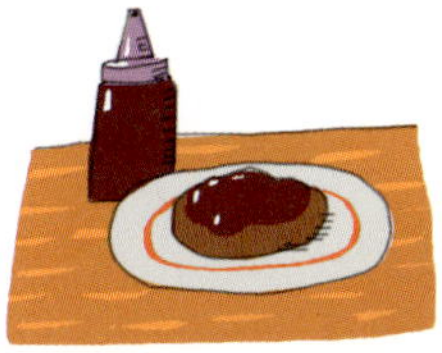

sauce

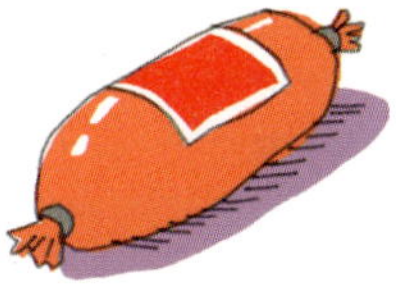

sausage

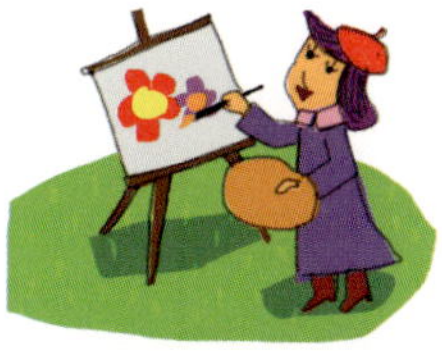

draw

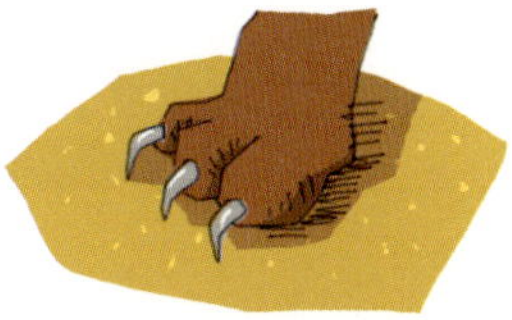

paw

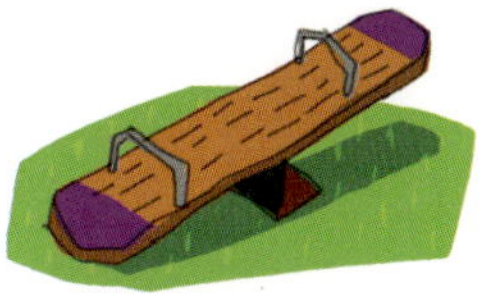

seesaw

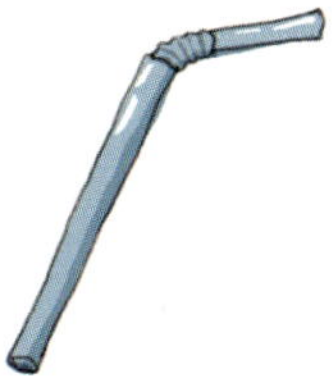

straw

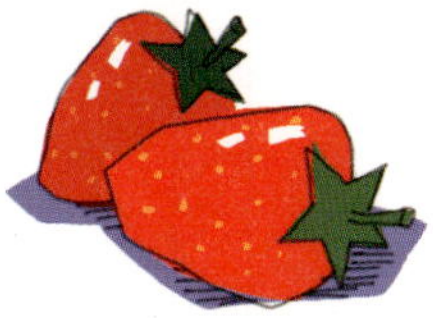

strawberry

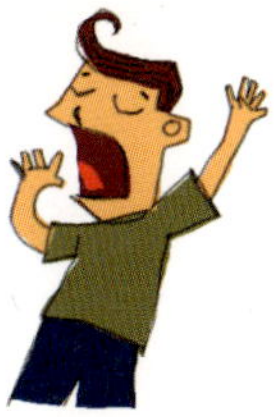

yawn

Practice

Sort and write the words according to the vowel sounds.

au

August

dinosaur

aw

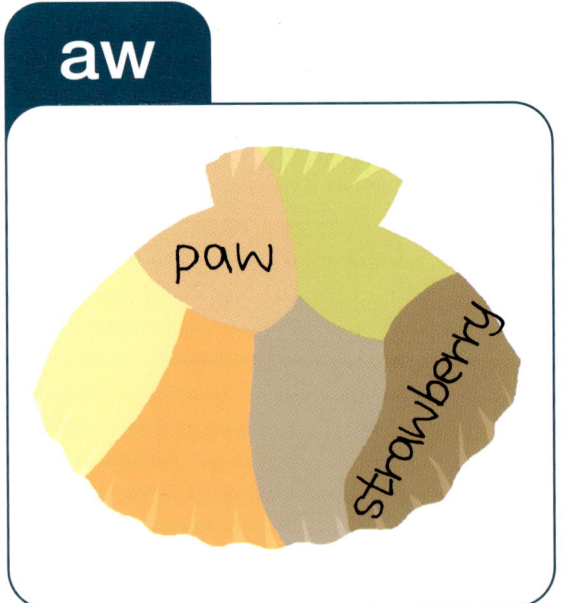

paw

strawberry

Listen, circle and write.

1

_____

- - - - - - - - - - - -

_____

2

_____

- - - - - - - - - - - -

_____

3

_____

- - - - - - - - - - - -

_____

4

_____

- - - - - - - - - - - -

_____

5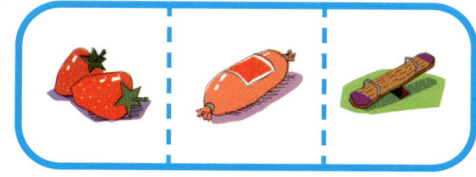

_____

- - - - - - - - - - - -

_____

6

_____

- - - - - - - - - - - -

_____

7

_____

- - - - - - - - - - - -

_____

8

_____

- - - - - - - - - - - -

_____

Read and find the correct sentence for the picture.

ⓐ

ⓑ

ⓒ

ⓓ

ⓔ

ⓕ

① The bee drinks with a straw. ☐

② The dinosaur sits on the stone. ☐

③ The man eats sausage with sauce. ☐

④ The kid draws a strawberry. ☐

⑤ The frogs play on the seesaw. ☐

⑥ Dad yawns on the bed. ☐

Circle the correct letters and write the word.

1
y
au aw
n

_____

2
sees
au aw

_____

3
s
aw au
ce

_____

4
dr
aw au

_____

5
Au Aw
gust

_____

6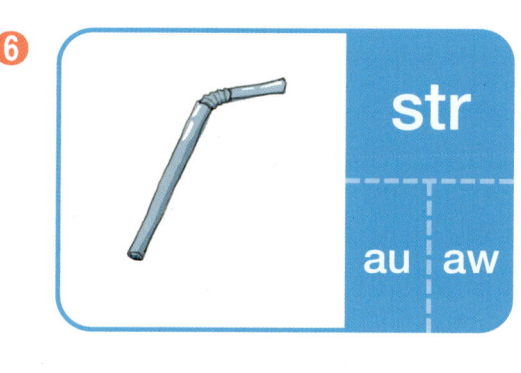
str
au aw

_____

23

Circle correct words and complete the story.

- A ![dinosaur] _____ and a sheep want to ride the seesaw.

- They sit on the ![seesaw] _____.

- But the ![seesaw] _____ doesn't go up and down.

- The ![dinosaur] _____ is big and heavy, but the sheep is small and light.

- The sheep brings her two more friends.

- Now, they can play on the ![seesaw] _____ and have fun.

Activity *chant*

Dinosaur, dinosaur
What do you draw?
I draw a sausage.

Dinosaur, dinosaur
What do you draw?
I draw strawberries.

Dinosaur, dinosaur
What do you draw?
I draw a seesaw.

It is snowing.
There is a snowman on the road.
A goat and a toad make it better.
The goat puts the yellow coat
on the snowman.
The toad puts the blue bowl
on the snowman.
They play with the snowman.

Listen and repeat.

b	**oa**	**t**
g	**oa**	**t**
b	**ow**	**l**
sn		**ow**

Match and write.

g	oat
b	ow
sn	oat
b	owl

Listen, point and repeat.

b**oa**t	c**oa**t	g**oa**t
r**oa**d	s**oa**p	t**oa**d
b**ow**l	elb**ow**	pill**ow**
sn**ow**	wind**ow**	yell**ow**

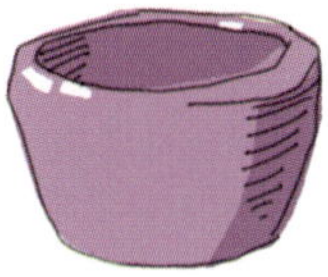

29

Practice

Sort and write the words according to the vowel sounds.

oa

soap

road

ow

bowl pillow

Listen, circle and write.

1

2

3

4

5

6

7

8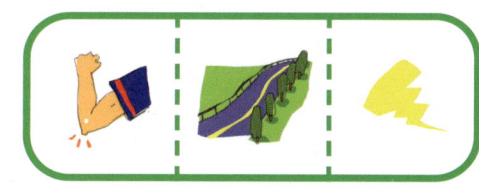

31

Read and find the correct sentence for the picture.

❶ The toad is in front of the window.

❷ The kid has a yellow coat.

❸ The truck is on the road.

❹ A bee is in the bowl.

❺ A goat eats grass and leaves.

❻ Mom washes the baby with soap.

Circle the correct letters and write the word.

❶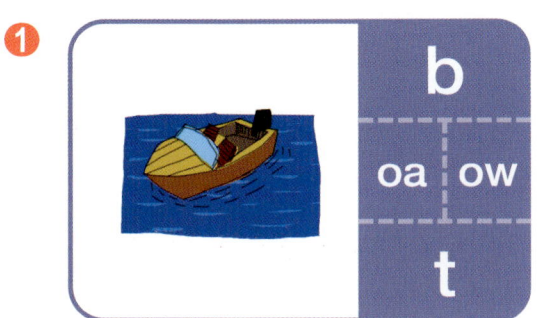

b
oa | ow
t

_____
- - - - - - - - - - - - -
_____

❷

g
oa | ow
t

_____
- - - - - - - - - - - - -
_____

❸

t
ow | oa
d

_____
- - - - - - - - - - - - -
_____

❹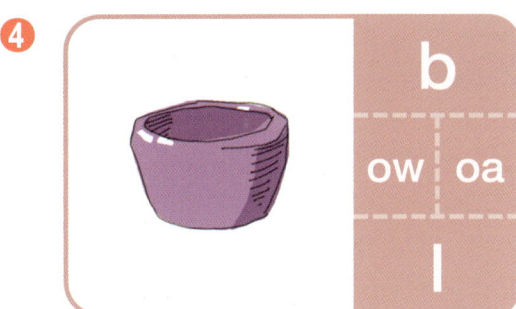

b
ow | oa
l

_____
- - - - - - - - - - - - -
_____

❺

pill
oa | ow

_____
- - - - - - - - - - - - -
_____

❻

c
oa | ow
t

_____
- - - - - - - - - - - - -
_____

Circle correct words and complete the story.

1 toad / towd

2 boal / bowl

3 snow / snoa

4 cowt / coat

5 road / rowd

6 goat / gowt

- It's _____ing.

- There is a snowman on the _____.

- A _____ and a _____ make it better.

- The goat puts the yellow _____ on the snowman.

- The toad puts the blue _____ on the snowman.

- They play with the _____man.

Activity *chant*

Look at the window.

It's snowing out side.

The goat makes a pillow with snow.

The toad makes a bowl with snow.

The fox makes a bed with snow.

The dog makes a gate with snow.

They make a snow house.

Five gray mice and a dog play
together in the pail.
The mice want to get out of the pail.
But they can't get out of it.
The dog can't help them
because his tail is short.
It's starting to rain.
The pail is full of water.
Now, the mice can reach
the top of the pail.

Listen and repeat.

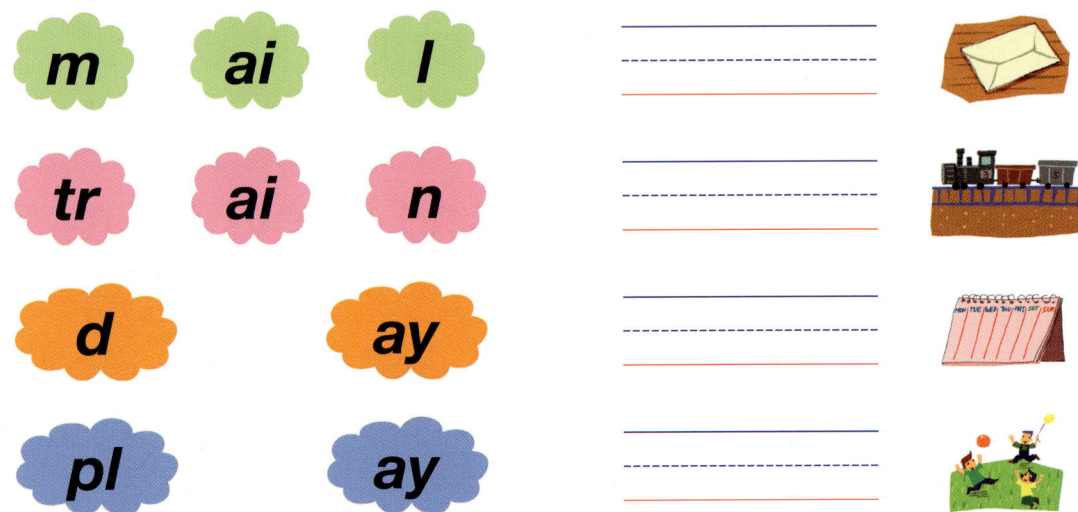

m **ai** **l**

tr **ai** **n**

d **ay**

pl **ay**

Match and write.

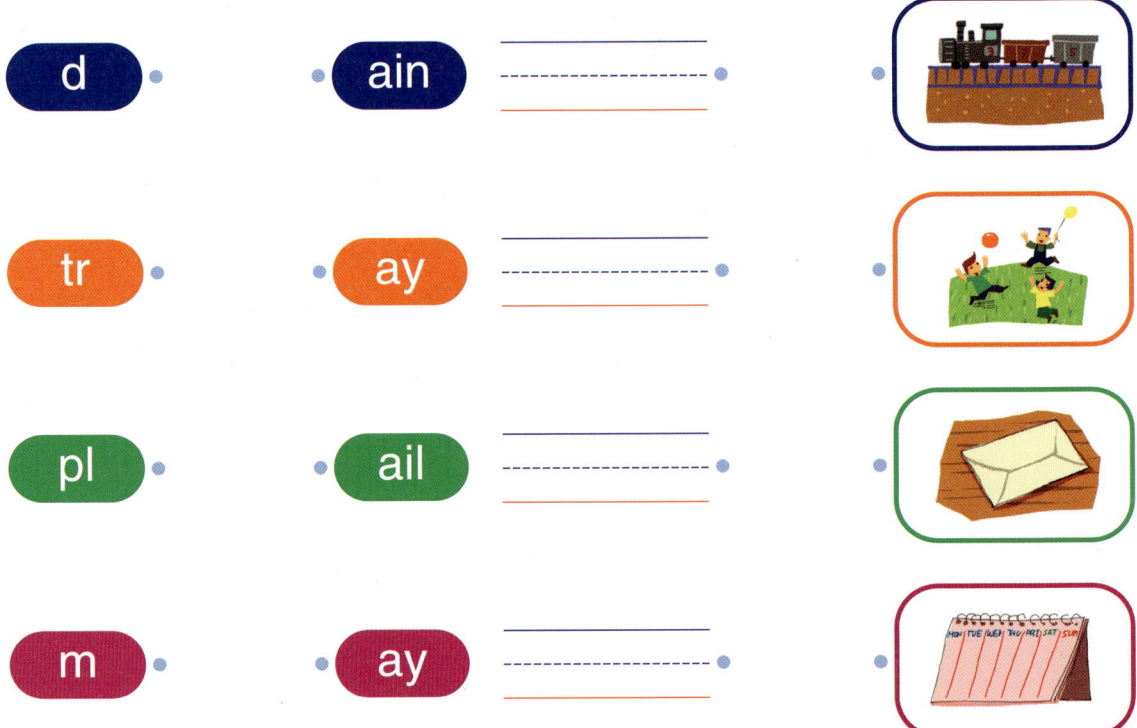

d · · ain

tr · · ay

pl · · ail

m · · ay

Listen, point and repeat.

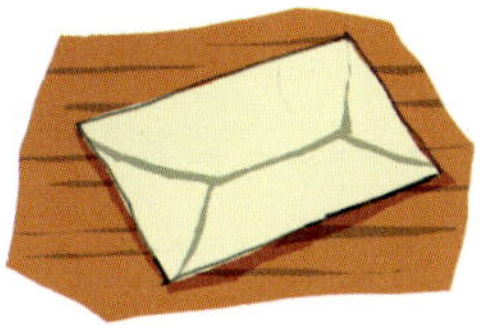

m**ai**l

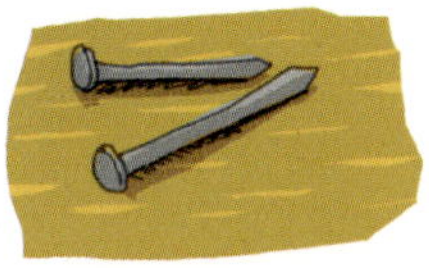

n**ai**l

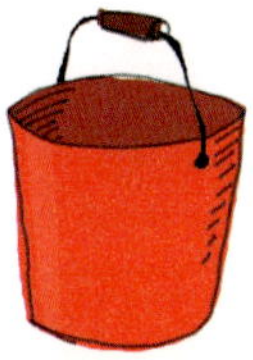

p**ai**l

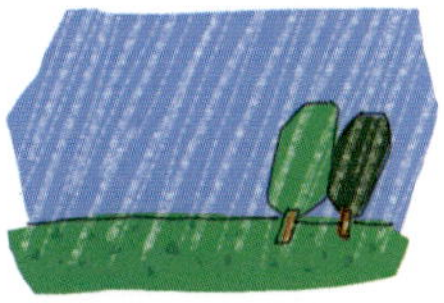

r**ai**n

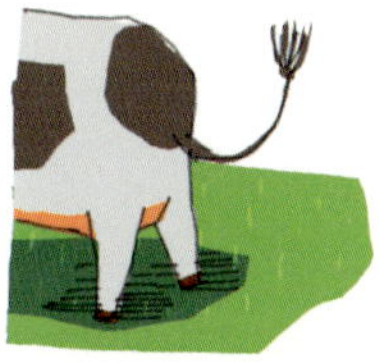

t**ai**l

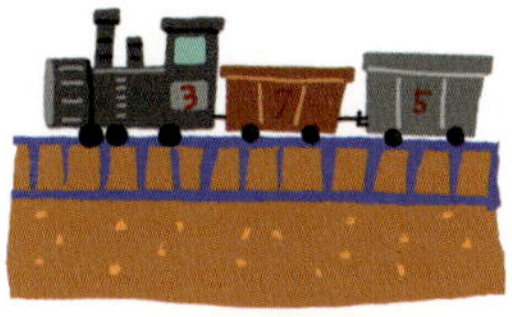

tr**ai**n

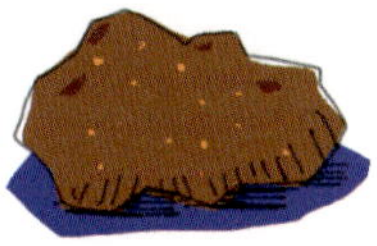

cl**ay**

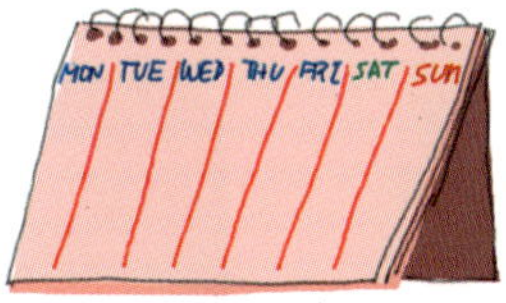

d**ay**

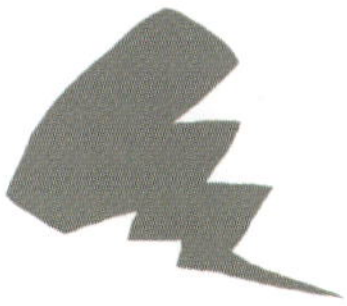

gr**ay**

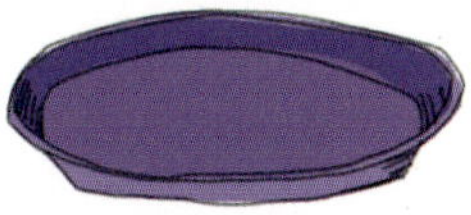

tr**ay**

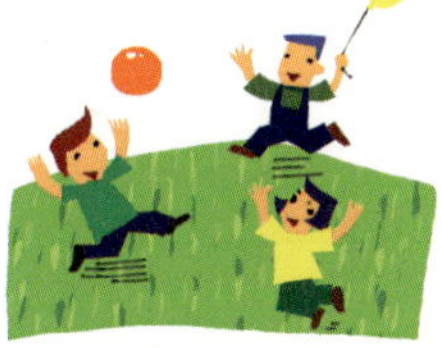

pl**ay**

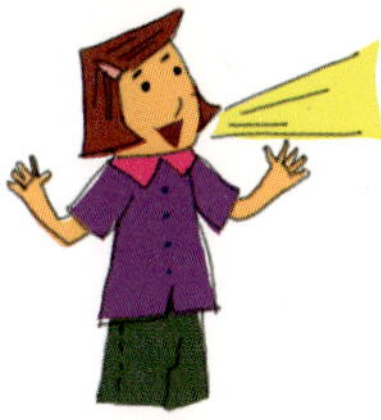

s**ay**

39

Practice

Sort and write the words according to the vowel sounds.

   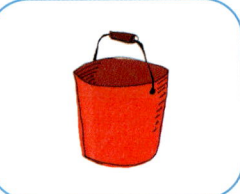

ai

rain nail

ay

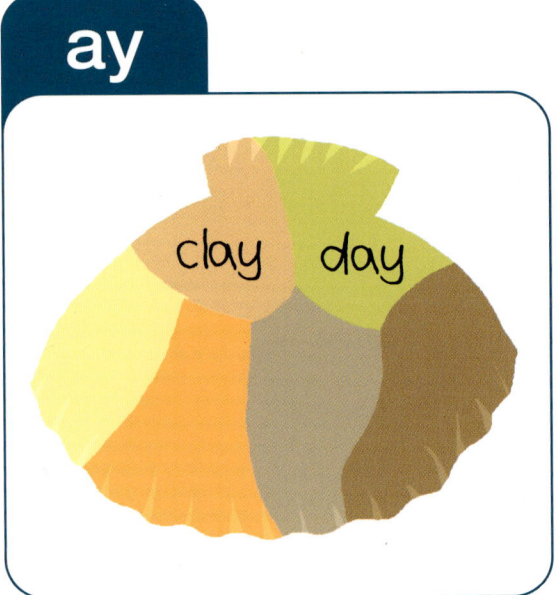

clay day

Listen, circle and write.

①

_____

- - - - - - - - - - - - -

_____

②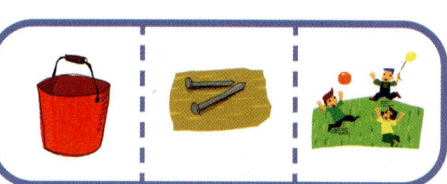

_____

- - - - - - - - - - - - -

_____

③

_____

- - - - - - - - - - - - -

_____

④

_____

- - - - - - - - - - - - -

_____

⑤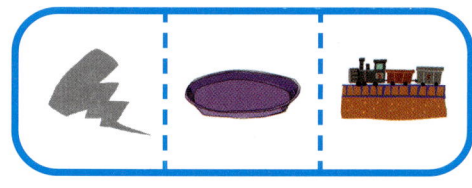

_____

- - - - - - - - - - - - -

_____

⑥

_____

- - - - - - - - - - - - -

_____

⑦

_____

- - - - - - - - - - - - -

_____

⑧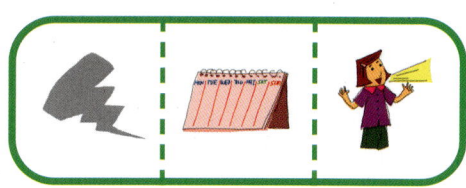

_____

- - - - - - - - - - - - -

_____

41

Read and find the correct sentence for the picture.

ⓐ

ⓑ

ⓒ

ⓓ

ⓔ

ⓕ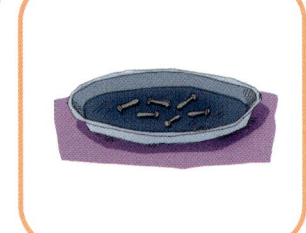

1 The kid plays with the top. ☐

2 The tree is in the rain. ☐

3 The gray nails are on the tray. ☐

4 There is a pail on the boat. ☐

5 The man makes a train with clay. ☐

6 The fox has a yellow tail. ☐

Circle the correct letters and write the word.

1

r
ai | ay
n

_____

2

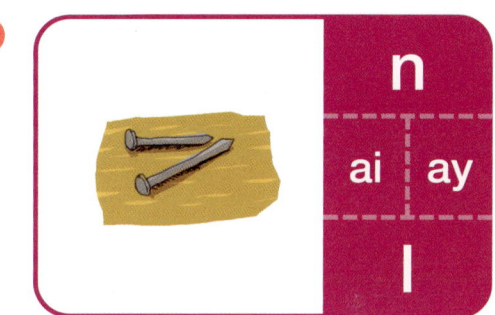

n
ai | ay
l

_____

3

pl
ay | ai

_____

4

m
ay | ai
l

_____

5

tr
ai | ay
n

_____

6

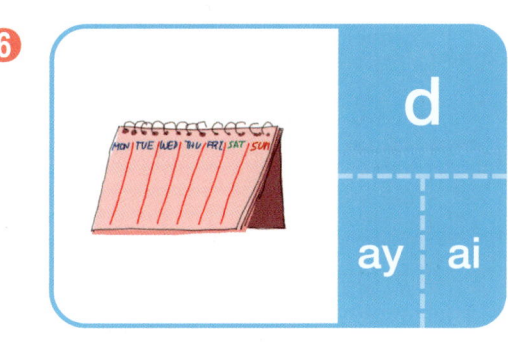

d
ay | ai

_____

43

Circle correct words and complete the story.

❶ tail | tayl

❷ grai | gray

❸ rayn | rain

❹ payl | pail

❺ plai | play

❻ clai | clay

- Five gray mice and a dog _____ together in the pail.

- The mice want to get out of the _____ .

- But they can't get out of it.

- The dog can't help them because his _____ is short.

- It's starting to _____ . The _____ is full of water.

- Now, the mice can reach the top of the _____ .

44

Activity *chant*

What do you see in the rain?

I see the man with the mail.

What do you see in the rain?

I see the train with clay.

What do you see in the rain?

I see the gray mice with the tray.

What do you see in the rain?

I see the pail by the window.

A boy drops the coins in the soil.
Two toads find the coins.
The toads play with the coins.
The boy points to the coins and says,
"The coins are mine!"
The toads say, "These are our toys.
Then let's play together."
They join together
and share the coins.

Sounds

Listen and repeat.

Match and write.

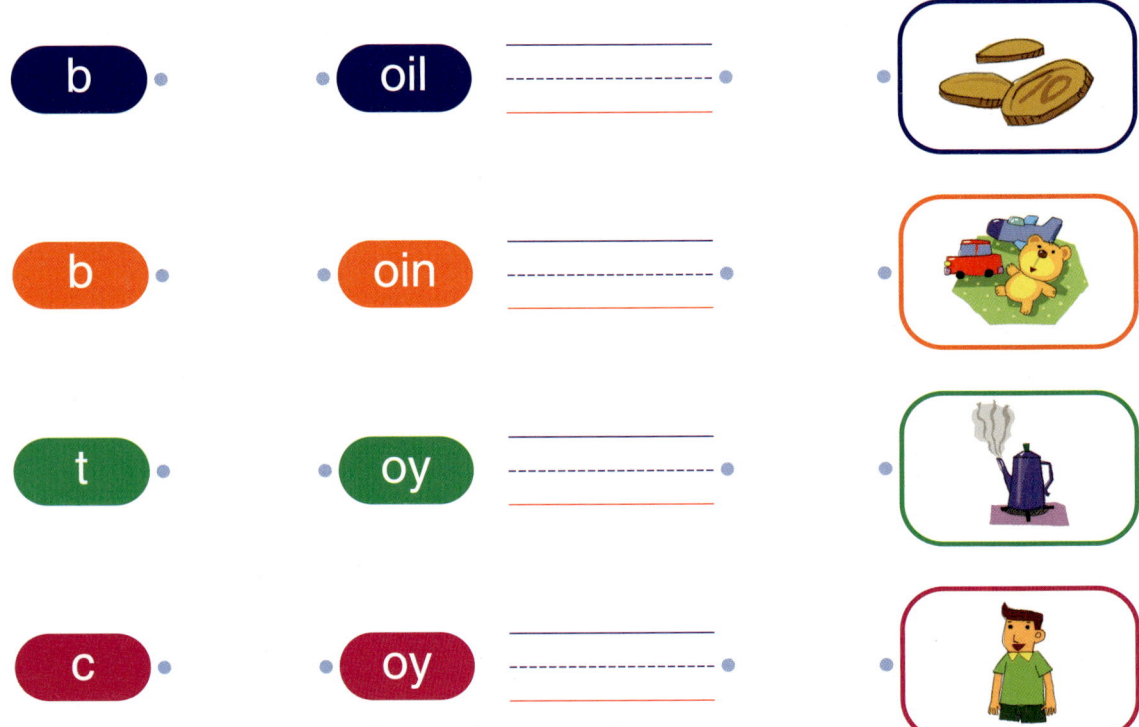

Listen, point and repeat.

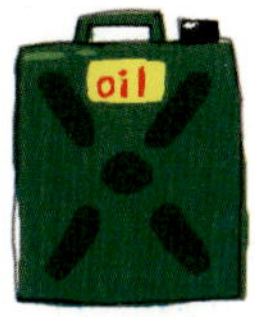

oil

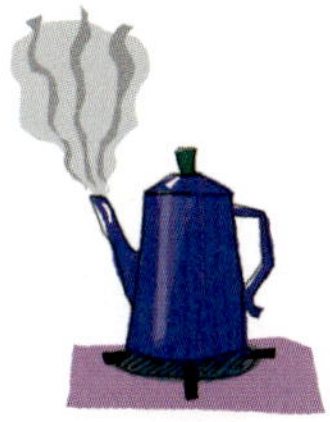

boil

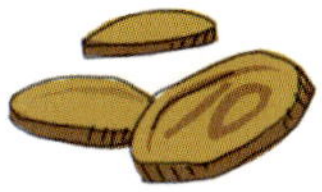

coin

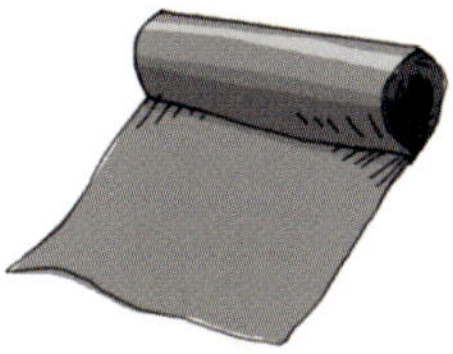

foil

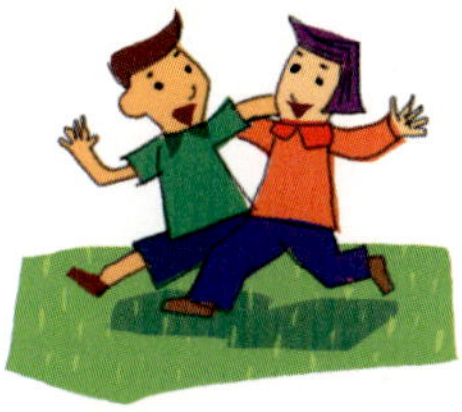

join

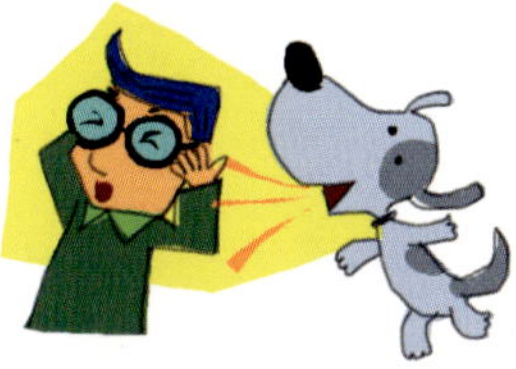

noise

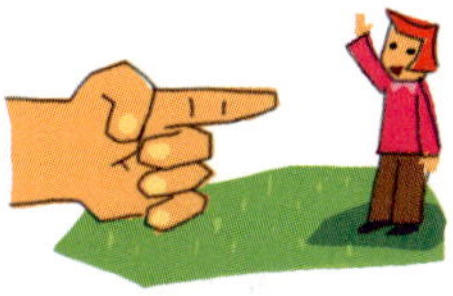

point

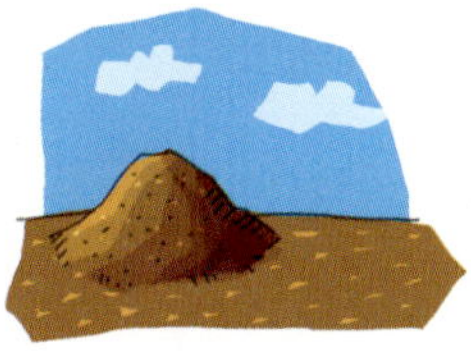

soil

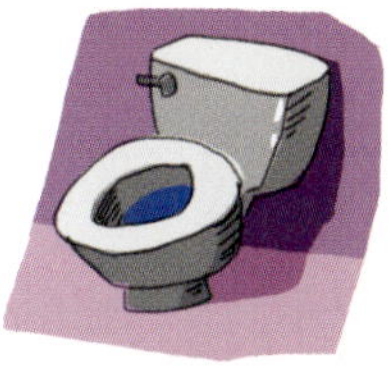

toilet

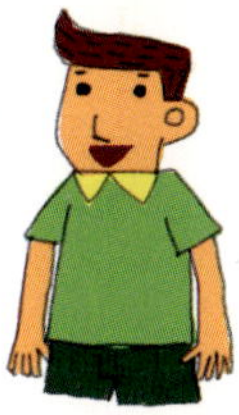

boy

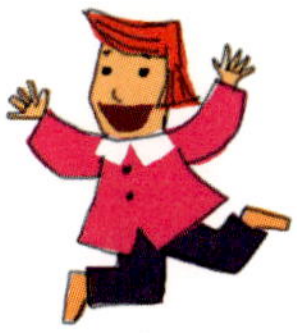

joy

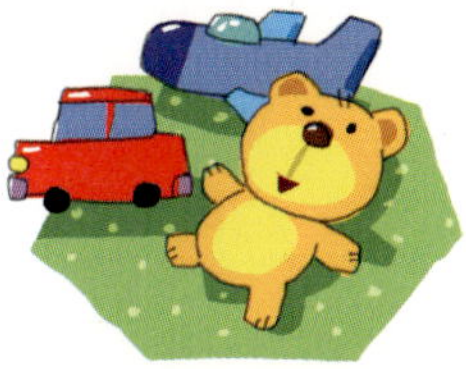

toy

Practice

Sort and write the words according to the vowel sounds.

oi

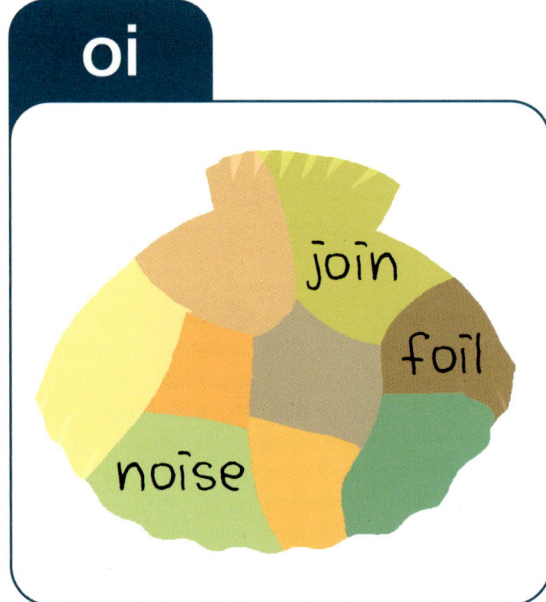

join
foil
noise

oy

joy

Listen, circle and write.

1

_____

2

_____

3

_____

4

_____

5

_____

6

_____

7

_____

8

_____

Read and find the correct sentence for the picture.

ⓐ 　　ⓑ 　　ⓒ

ⓓ 　　ⓔ 　　ⓕ

❶ The coins are on the tray. ☐

❷ The man points to the boat. ☐

❸ The boy plays with the toy. ☐

❹ The dog puts the bone in the soil. ☐

❺ Mom boils the eggs. ☐

❻ The oil is on the coat. ☐

Circle the correct letters and write the word.

1

b
oi | oy
l

_____

2

c
oi | oy
n

_____

3

t
oy | oi

_____

4

j
oy | oi
n

_____

5

oi | oy
l

_____

6

b
oi | oy

_____

Circle correct words and complete the story.

- A boy drops the coins in the  _____ .

- Two toads find the _____s.

- The toads play with the _____s.

- The boy _____s to the _____s and says,

  "The _____ s are mine!"

- The toads say, "These are our toys. Then let's play together."

- They _____ together and share the _____s.

Activity *chant*

Oil oil, oil in the pan.

Boil boil, boil the eggs.

Coins coins, coins in the piggy bank.

Soil soil rose in the soil.

Noise noise, noise in the class.

Toy toy, boy with the toy.

Join join, join for the joy.

Color the words green that have the same vowel sounds.
Color all of the other words yellow.

coin coat

boil pail

draw
seesaw

tail
toilet

sheep
tree

pillow
snow

rain
road

play
gray

boil
coin

bowl
window

snow
straw

bean eat

say
toy

tea
sea

fault
feet

yawn yellow

Listen, read and complete the crossword puzzle.

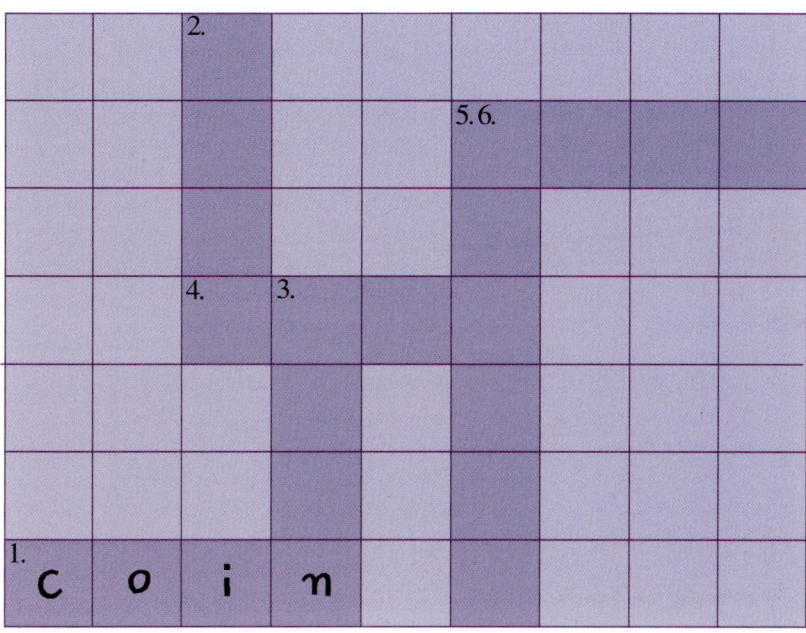

Down

2. The kid has a yellow  .

3. The boy is in the  .

5. The frogs play on the  .

Across

1. The  is on the tray.

4. The man sleeps under the .

6. Mom washes the baby with  .

57

Review 1

Listen and circle the word you hear.

r	f	s	e	a	g	u
w	a	e	g	r	a	y
s	t	o	b	j	e	a
i	a	s	t	o	s	w
b	i	o	y	b	w	n
e	l	a	l	e	a	l
e	t	p	o	w	m	a

Match the sentence with the picture.

ⓐ The boy eats sausage and strawberries.

ⓑ The boy plays with the toy train.

ⓒ The boy puts the toys in the pail.

ⓓ The boy sleeps with a pillow.

This is a contest for the best clown.
The first clown has a red nose
and a big mouth.
The second clown has a smart mouse.
The mouse can count numbers.
The third clown has a funny brown gown.
They can make you laugh.

Sounds

Listen and repeat.

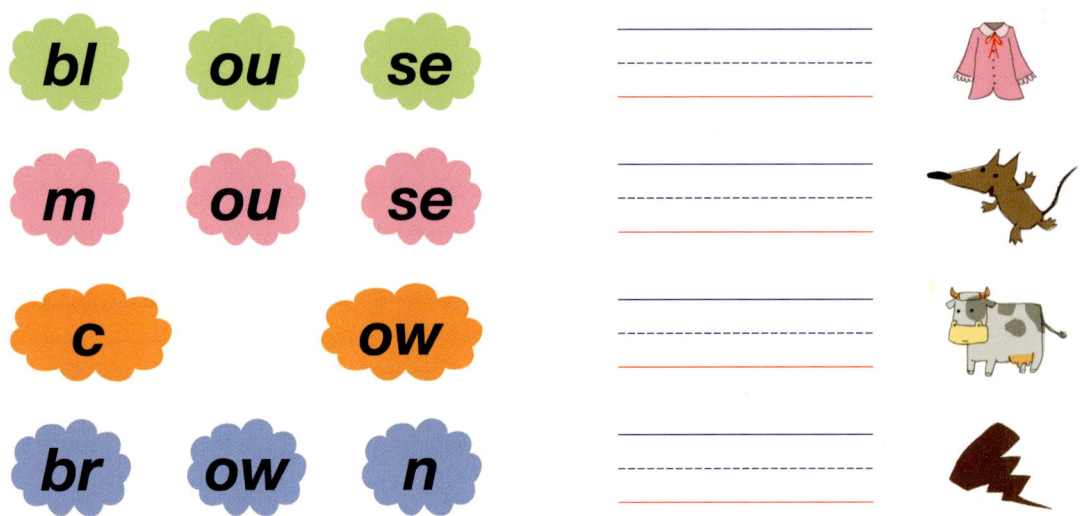

bl	ou	se
m	ou	se
c		ow
br	ow	n

Match and write.

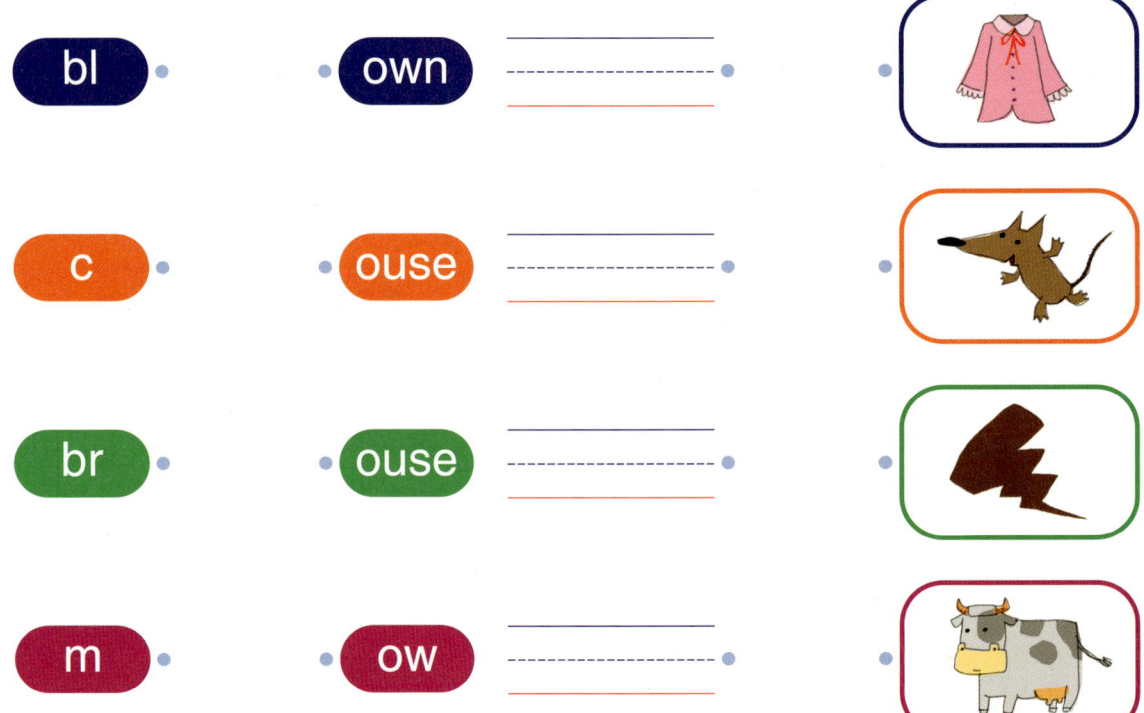

bl •	• own	
c •	• ouse	
br •	• ouse	
m •	• ow	

Listen, point and repeat.

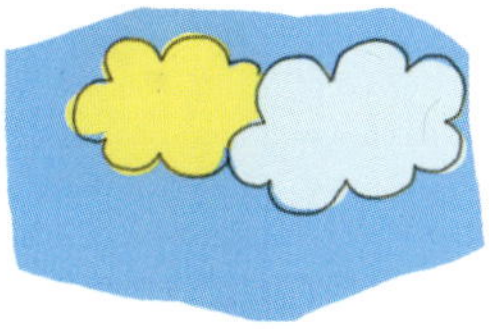

cloud	count	bl**ou**se
h**ou**se	m**ou**se	m**ou**th
c**ow**	g**ow**n	**ow**l
br**ow**n	cr**ow**n	cl**ow**n

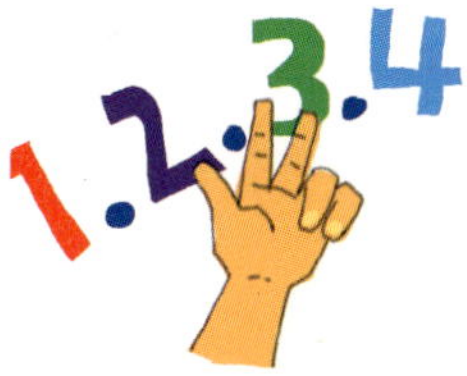

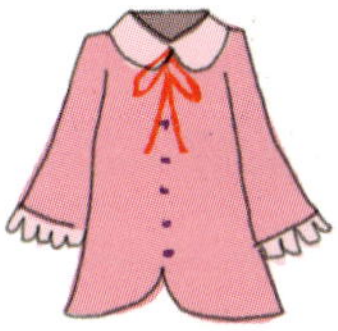

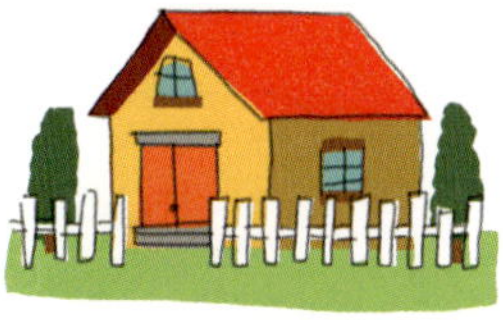

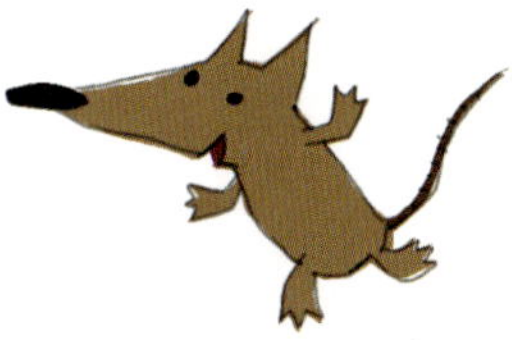

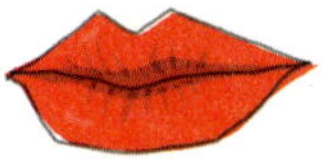

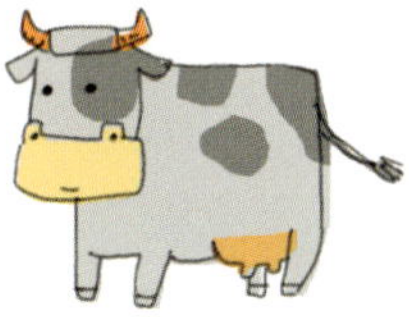

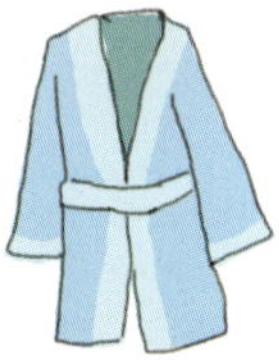

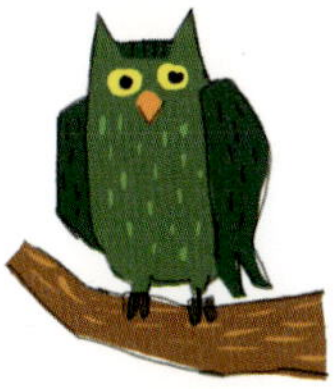

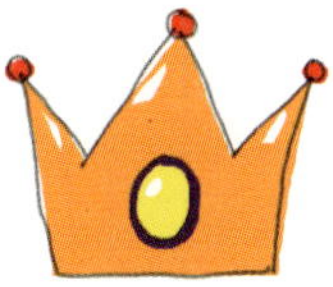

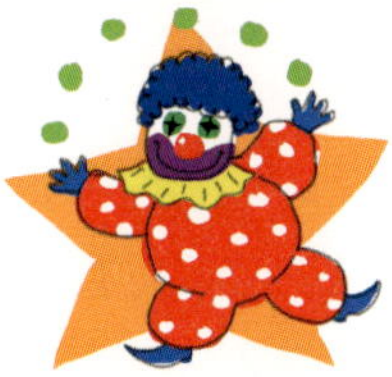

Practice

Sort and write the words according to the vowel sounds.

ow

cow

brown

ou

mouth

cloud

Listen, circle and write.

1

_____

- - - - - - - - - - - - - -

_____

2

_____

- - - - - - - - - - - - - -

_____

3

_____

- - - - - - - - - - - - - -

_____

4

_____

- - - - - - - - - - - - - -

_____

5

_____

- - - - - - - - - - - - - -

_____

6

_____

- - - - - - - - - - - - - -

_____

7

_____

- - - - - - - - - - - - - -

_____

8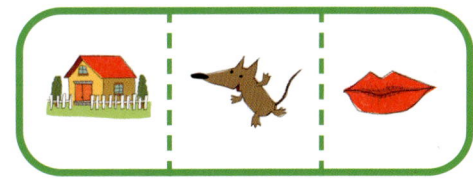

_____

- - - - - - - - - - - - - -

_____

Read and find the correct sentence for the picture.

ⓐ  ⓑ  ⓒ

ⓓ  ⓔ  ⓕ

❶ The mouse counts the cats. ☐

❷ The owl is on the tree. ☐

❸ The clown has a big mouth. ☐

❹ Mom has a yellow blouse. ☐

❺ The dog has a brown house. ☐

❻ The cow has a crown. ☐

Circle the correct letters and write the word.

1

bl
ow | ou
se

2

h
ow | ou
se

3

cr
ou | ow
n

4

ow | ou
l

5

g
ou | ow
n

6

c
ou | ow
nt

Circle correct words and complete the story.

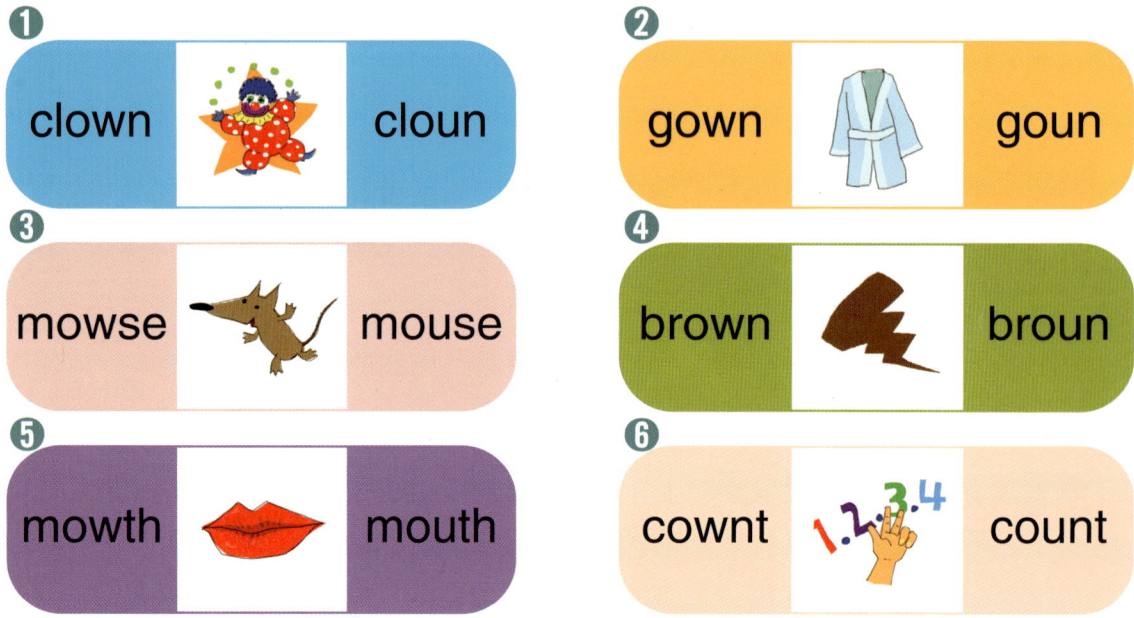

❶ clown   cloun

❷ gown   goun

❸ mowse   mouse

❹ brown   broun

❺ mowth   mouth

❻ cownt   count

- This is a contest for the best  _____.

- The first clown has a red nose and a big  _____.

- The second clown has a smart  _____.

- The mouse can  _____ numbers.

- The third clown has a funny  _____ _____.

- They can make you laugh.

Activity *chant*

How many cows are there?
One two three

There are four cows.
One two three four

How many owls are there?
One two three

There are five owls.
One two three four five

How many clowns are there?
One two three

There are six clowns.
One two three four five six

The blue bird and the purple turtle look at the singer. The blue bird says, " The singer is cool. I want to be a singer someday. What do you want to be, turtle?" The purple turtle says, "I want to be a nurse. I like to help others." They have great dreams.

Listen and repeat.

Match and write.

b   er

sing   urtle

t   ird

72

Listen, point and repeat.

b**ir**d

g**ir**l

sk**ir**t

sh**ir**t

dinn**er**

sing**er**

teach**er**

socc**er**

c**ur**l

n**ur**se

p**ur**ple

t**ur**tle

73

Sort and write the words according to the vowel sounds.

ir	er	ur
girl	dinner	curl

Listen, circle and write.

 1

_____
- -
_____

2

_____
- -
_____

3

_____
- -
_____

4

_____
- -
_____

5

_____
- -
_____

6

_____
- -
_____

7

_____
- -
_____

8

_____
- -
_____

Read and find the correct sentence for the picture.

ⓐ    ⓑ    ⓒ

ⓓ    ⓔ    ⓕ

❶ The girl with curls has a yellow skirt. ☐

❷ The bird is on the tree. ☐

❸ The boy plays soccer. ☐

❹ The kid points to the singer. ☐

❺ The teacher counts the coins. ☐

❻ The nurse drinks some tea. ☐

Circle the correct letters and write the word.

1

sk

ir ┊ er

t

_____

2

teach

ir ┊ er

_____

3

dinn

er ┊ ur

_____

4

n

er ┊ ur

se

_____

5

socc

ir ┊ er

_____

6

sing

er ┊ ur

_____

Circle correct words and complete the story.

① singur / singer

② nirse / nurse

③ burd / bird

④ turtle / tertle

⑤ purple / pirple

⑥ gurl / girl

- The blue _____ and the purple turtle look at the singer.

- The blue bird says, "The _____ is cool. I want to be

  a _____ someday. What do you want to be, turtle?"

  The _____ turtle says, "I want to be a _____.

  I like to help others"

- They have great dreams.

Activity *chant*

The kid has curly hair.
The girl has a yellow skirt.
The boy has a blue shirt.
The singer sings with a bird.
The teacher has a purple turtle.
The purple turtle wants them
to play soccer all together.

Unit 8 Double Letters ar or

A little girl and her mom
sit on the bench in the park.
The little girl wants to go to the stars.
"Mom, can I go to the stars by car?"
Mom says, "No, you can't go there by
car." The little girl asks again,
"Can I go to the stars by train?"
"No. you can't go there by train.
You can go to the stars
by the white horse with a horn."

Listen and repeat.

c	ar	
p	ar	k
c	or	n
h	or	se

Match and write.

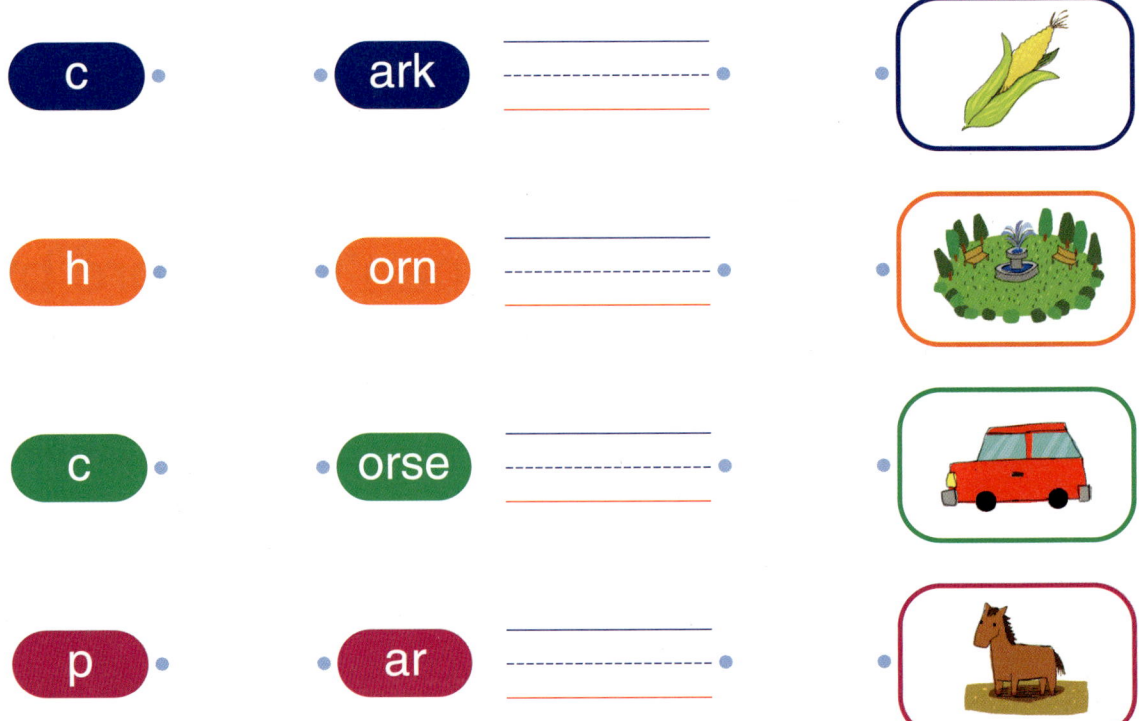

Listen, point and repeat.

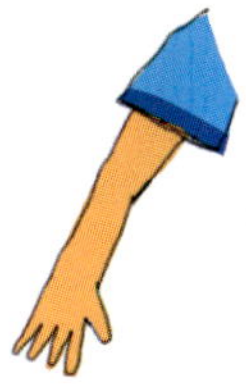

a**r**m	c**a**r	b**a**rn
p**a**rk	st**a**r	y**a**rn
c**o**rn	f**o**rk	h**o**rn
h**o**rse	sh**o**rt	st**o**rm

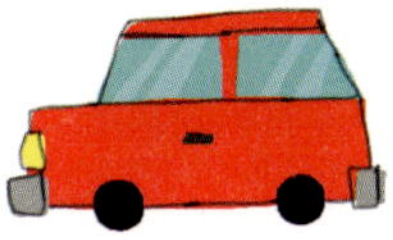

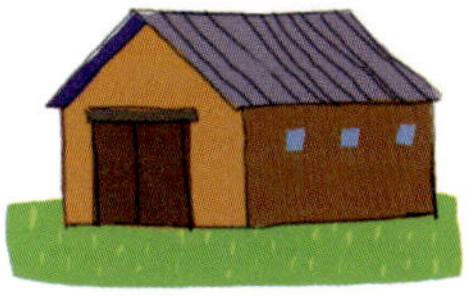

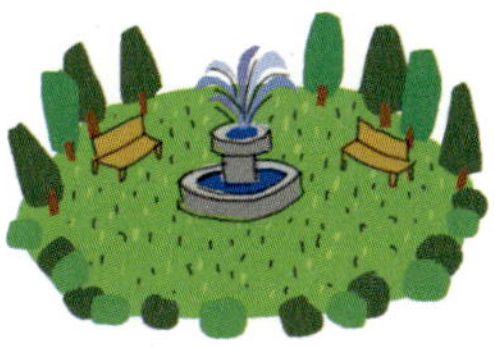

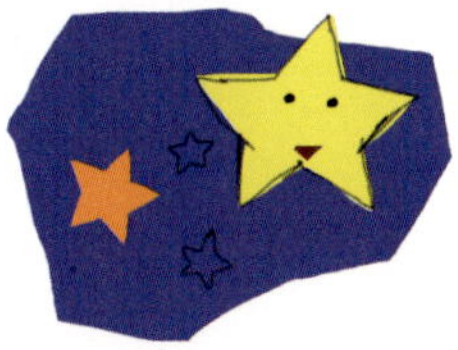

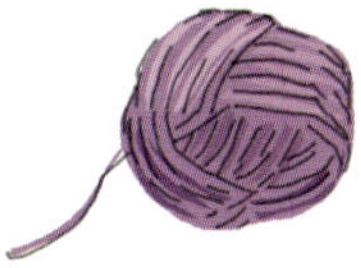

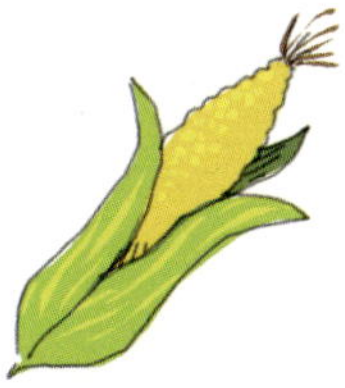

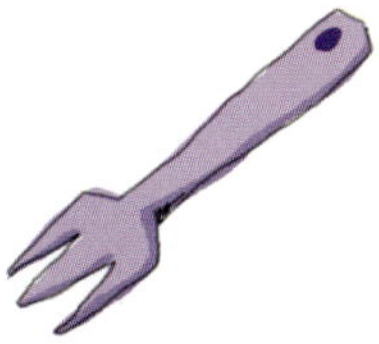

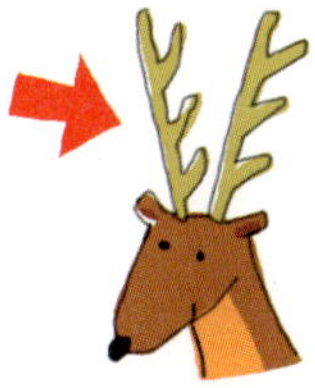

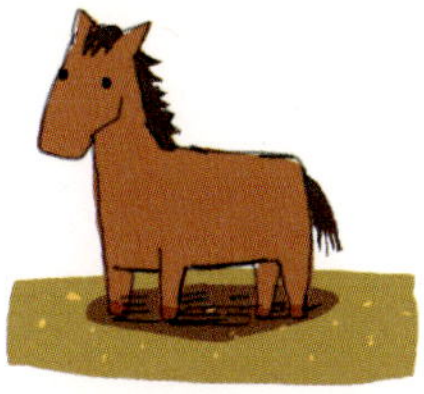

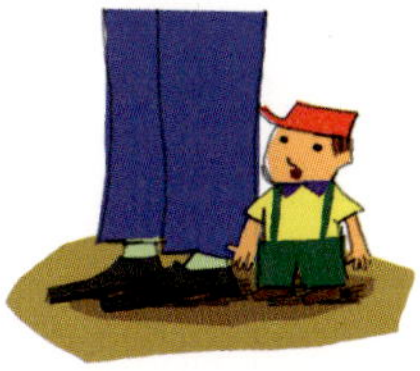

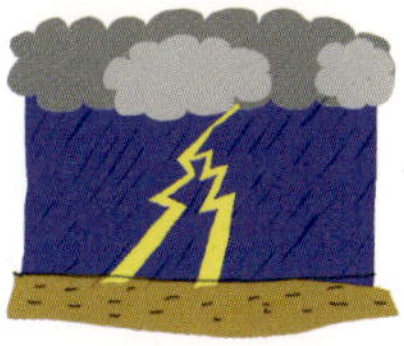

Practice

Sort and write the words according to the vowel sounds.

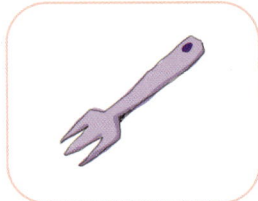   

ar

star

yarn

or

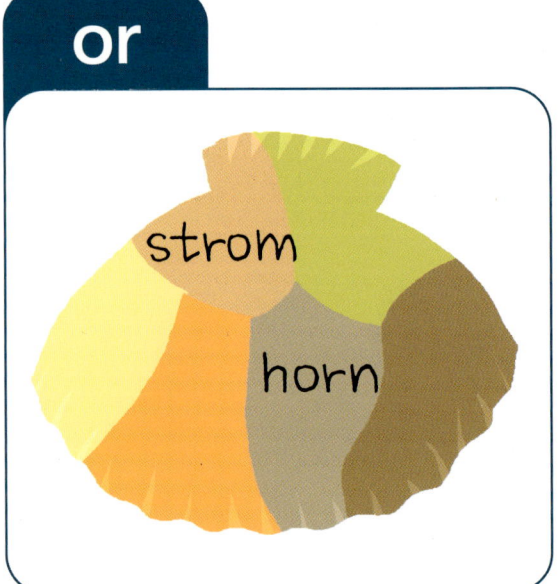

strom

horn

84

Listen, circle and write.

1.

2.

3.

4.

5.

6.

7.

8.

Read and find the correct sentence for the picture.

ⓐ  ⓑ  ⓒ

ⓓ  ⓔ  ⓕ

1 The girl has dinner with a fork. ☐

2 The goat has horns. ☐

3 The boy likes the toy car. ☐

4 The turtle has a short neck. ☐

5 The horse is by the barn. ☐

6 Mom has two corns. ☐

86

Circle the correct letters and write the word.

1

y
ar | or
n

_____

2
st
ar | or
m

_____

3

p
or | ar
k

_____

4

c
or | ar

_____

5

c
ar | or
n

_____

6

st
ar | or

_____

Word Search

Circle correct words and complete the story.

① car / cor

② star / stor

③ harn / horn

④ park / pork

⑤ harse / horse

⑥ carn / corn

- A little girl and her mom sit on the bench in the  _____ .

- The little girl wants to go to the  _____ s.

- "Mom, can I go to the stars by _____ ?

- Mom says, "No, you can't go there by _____ ."

- The little girl asks again, "Can I go to the _____ s by train?"

- "No, you can't go there by train. You can go to the stars

  by the white _____ with a _____ .

Activity *chant*

Star star in the Sky
Corn corn in the barn
Arm arm with the fork
Car car in the storm
Horse horse in the park
Horn horn on the goat
Yarn yarn for the sweater

There is a party at the zoo.
The mouse and the cow put
the balloons on the tree.
The cook turtle makes strawberry pie.
The goose and the duck
play in the pool.
The moon looks at them with a smile.
They have a great time at the party.

Listen and repeat.

Match and write.

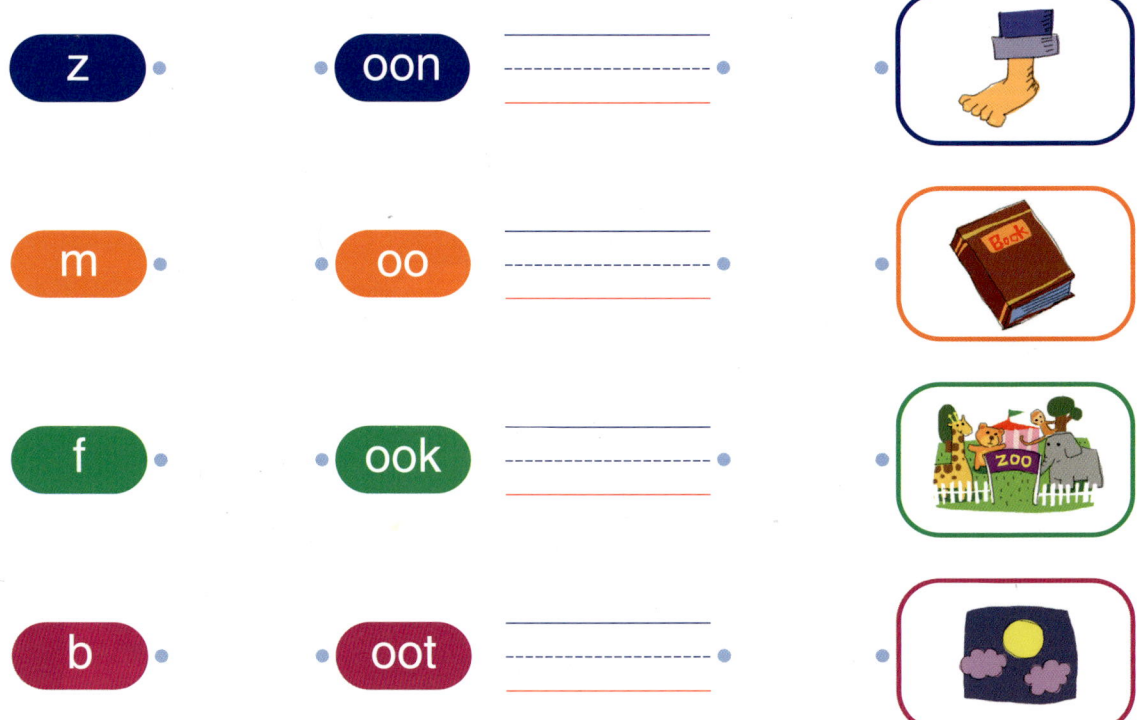

Listen, point and repeat.

book

cook

foot

look

wood

wool

balloon

boot

pool

goose

moon

zoo

Sort and write the words according to the vowel sounds.

OO [u]

book

wood

OO [u:]

balloon moon

Listen, circle and write.

1

_____

2

_____

3

_____

4

_____

5

_____

6

_____

7

_____

8

_____

Read and find the correct sentence for the picture.

ⓐ

ⓑ

ⓒ

ⓓ

ⓔ

ⓕ

1 The cook makes strawberry pie. ☐

2 The goose looks at the moon. ☐

3 The mouse blows up the balloon. ☐

4 The man makes a house with wood. ☐

5 The boy hurts his foot. ☐

6 The turtle reads the book. ☐

Circle the correct letters and write the word.

①

z
oo [u] | oo [u:]

----

②
w
oo [u] | oo [u:]
d

----

③
f
oo [u] | oo [u:]
t

----

④

l
oo [u] | oo [u:]
k

----

⑤
b
oo [u] | oo [u:]
k

----

⑥

b
oo [u] | oo [u:]
t

97

Word Search

Circle correct words and complete the story.

- There is a party at the  _____.

- The mouse and the cow put the  _____s on the tree.

- The _____ turtle makes strawberry pie.

- The goose and the duck play in the _____.

- The _____ looks at them with a smile.

- They have a great time at the party.

Activity *chant*

Book, book,
What shape are you?

I am rectangular.
I am rectangular.

Balloon, balloon,
What shape are you?

I am oval.
I am oval.

Moon, moon,
What shape are you?

I am round.
I am round.

Review 2

Color the words purple that have the same vowel sounds.
Color all of the other words gray.

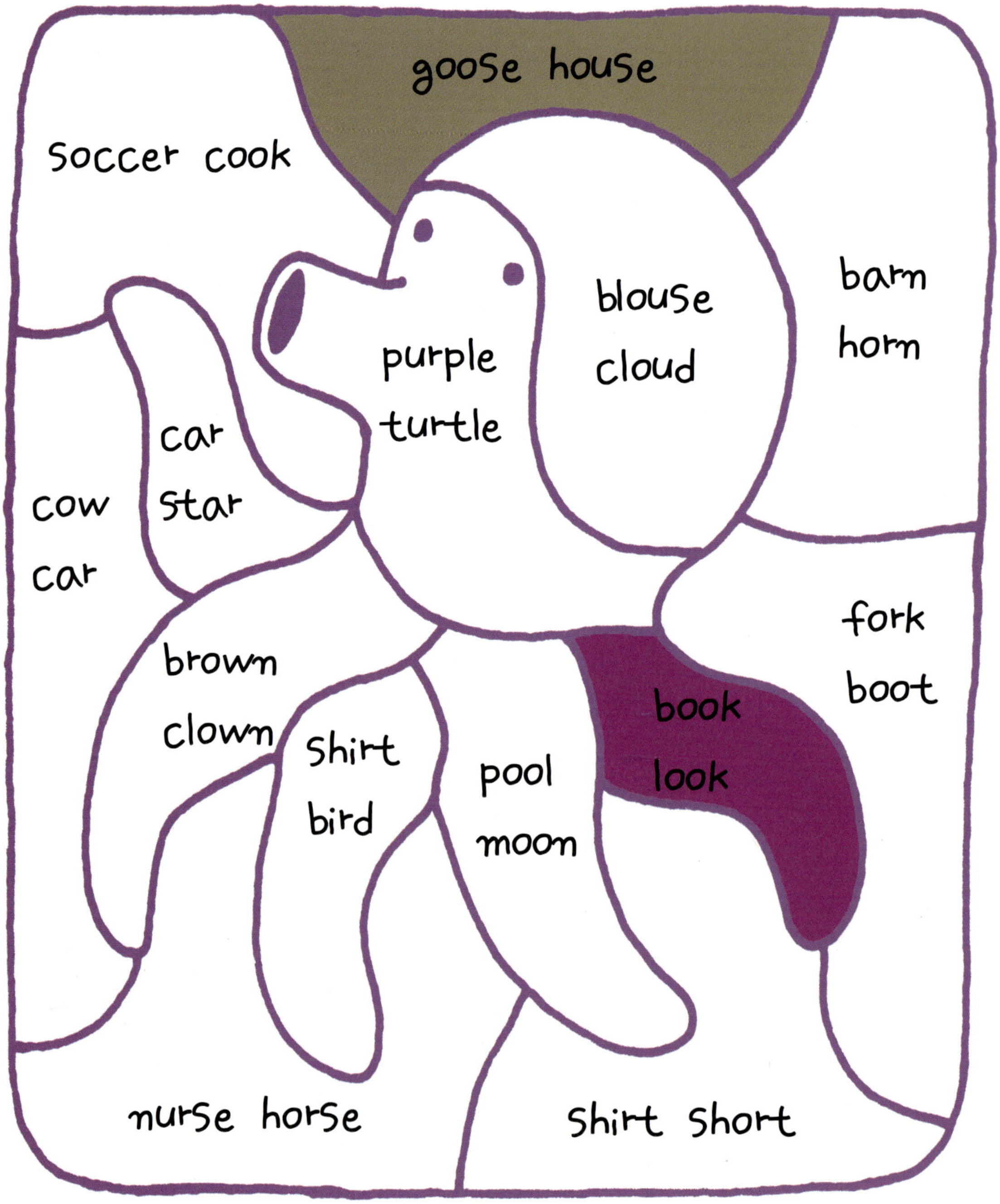

goose house

Soccer cook

blouse
cloud

barn
horn

purple
turtle

car
star

cow

car

fork
boot

brown

clown

book
look

Shirt
bird

pool
moon

nurse horse

Shirt Short

100

Listen, read and complete the crossword puzzle.

	1. m					5.		
2.	o		3.		4.			
	u							
	t		6.					
	h							
	7.							

Down

1. The clown has a big .

3. The boy plays .

5. A is in the bowl.

Across

2. The eats cheese.

4. The man makes a house with .

6. The has a crown.

7. The is on the tree.

101

Listen and circle the word you hear.

t	a	d	o	r	o	a	d
w	e	t	w	p	o	o	l
g	o	a	l	s	u	p	a
f	i	a	c	o	a	a	b
a	e	r	f	h	g	r	i
j	c	h	l	w	e	k	m
l	o	o	k	c	k	r	k
n	u	r	s	t	o	o	k

Match the sentence with the picture.

ⓐ There is an owl on the tree.

ⓑ The girl makes a house with wood for the owl.

ⓒ The owl makes strawberry pie for the girl.

ⓓ The owl and the girl look at the moon

and the stars.

Test

Listen and check.

 ①

a  b  c ✓

② a  b  c

③ a  b  c

④ a  b  c

⑤ a  b  c

⑥ a  b  c

7 ow

8 oo

9 ar

10 oi

11 oa

12 ea

Test

Listen and write.

1 The kid _point_ s to the _singer_.

2 Mom has a _____ _____.

3 The man makes a _____

with _____.

4 The _____ is on the _____.

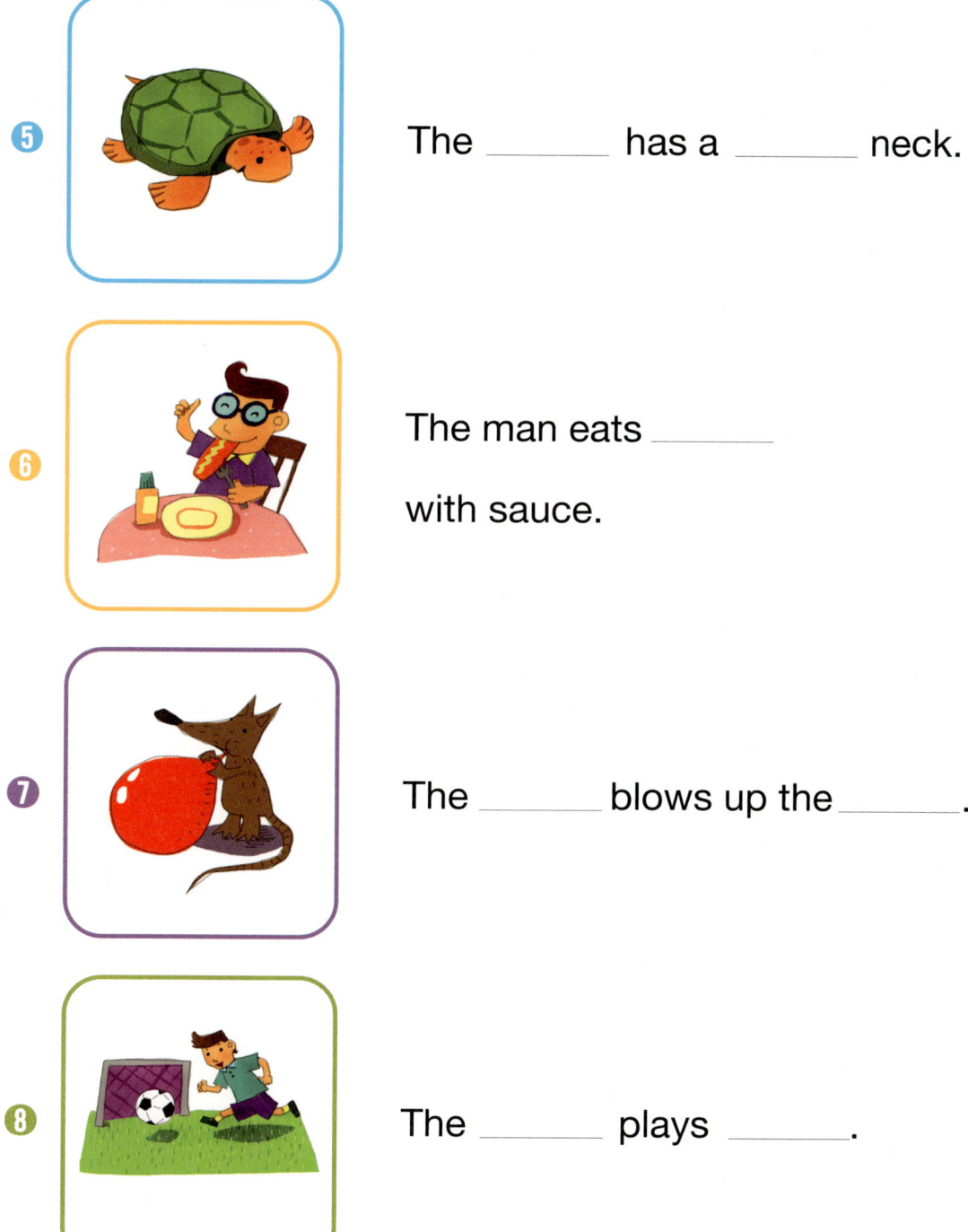

5 The _____ has a _____ neck.

6 The man eats _____

with sauce.

7 The _____ blows up the _____.

8 The _____ plays _____.

Test

Look and match.

1 · · (horse)

2 · · (strawberries)

3 · · (lips)

4 · · (coat)

5 · · (book)

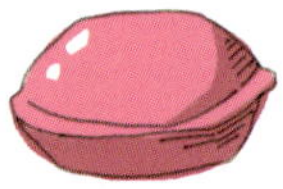

Listen and unscramble.

❶ rete

1. tree

❷ atog

2.

❸ nwos

3.

❹ noci

4.

8.

❽ nomo

5.

❺ trasw

❻ ˈsuoeh

❼ rokf

6.

7.

Activity

Follow the path that has the right match.

truck · toy · flag · clam

corn · blouse · park · sauce

frog · bird · glass · boil

tray · boat · mouse · drive

plane · bee · ski

Find and circle the words.

m	u	t	s	r	a	n	t
o	c	a	f	i	Y	c	o
u	l	b	o	l	n	k	a
t	e	d	n	a	d	g	d
h	p	u	p	l	a	Y	k
s	n	c	l	o	w	n	m
o	i	k	t	h	b	l	Y
u	w	c	b	r	u	s	h

Complete the crossword puzzle.

Across

2  4  6  8

					2.3.		5.	1.
			4.5.					
	7.							
6.								
	8.							

Down

1  3  5  7

Answer Key

8p

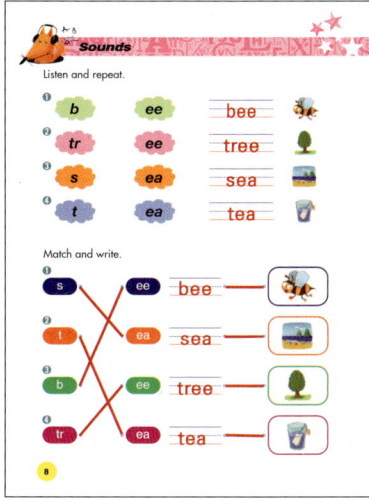

11p

14p

❶ leaf
❷ feed
❸ bean
❹ sheep
❺ tea
❻ bee

sheep
tea
sheep / leaf
bee
sheep / bee

10p

ee

sheep
feet
sleep
tree

ea

bean
eat
leaf
meat

12p

❶ e
❷ c
❸ f
❹ b
❺ a
❻ d

13p

❶ ee / bee
❷ ea / bean
❸ ea / tea
❹ ee / tree
❺ ea / eat
❻ ee / feet

18p

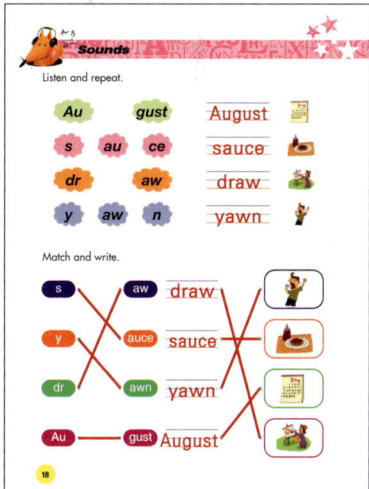

Answer Key

20p

au

Autumn

sauce

sausage

fault

aw

straw

seesaw

yawn

draw

21p

22p

❶ f

❷ d

❸ a

❹ e

❺ c

❻ b

23p

❶ aw / yawn

❷ aw / seesaw

❸ au / sauce

❹ aw / draw

❺ Au / August

❻ aw / straw

24p

❶ dinosaur

❷ seesaw

❸ sausage

❹ paw

❺ draw

❻ straw

dinosaur

seesaw

seesaw

dinosaur

seesaw

28p

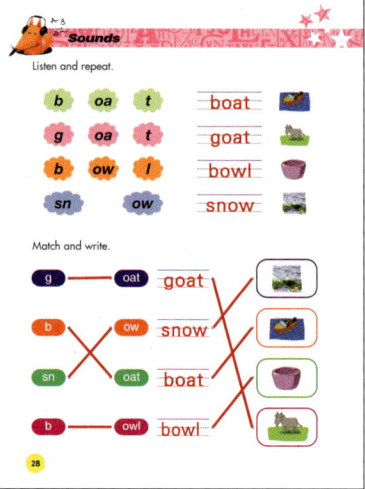

30p

oa

goat

toad

boat

coat

ow

elbow

yellow

snow

window

31p

32p

❶ b

❷ d

❸ f

❹ a

❺ e

❻ c

33p

❶ oa / boat
❷ oa / goat
❸ oa / toad
❹ ow / bowl
❺ ow / pillow
❻ oa / coat

34p

❶ toad
❷ bowl
❸ snow
❹ coat
❺ road
❻ goat

snow
road
goat toad
coat
bowl
snow

38p

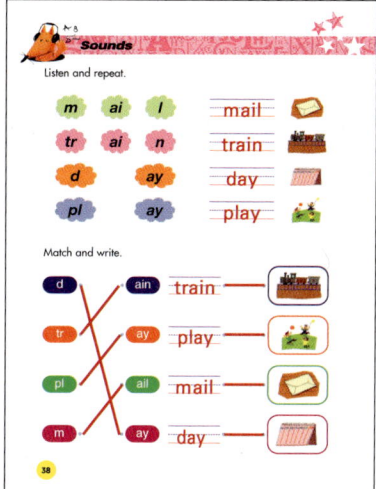

40p

ai
train
mail
tail
pail

ay
say
gray
tray
play

41p

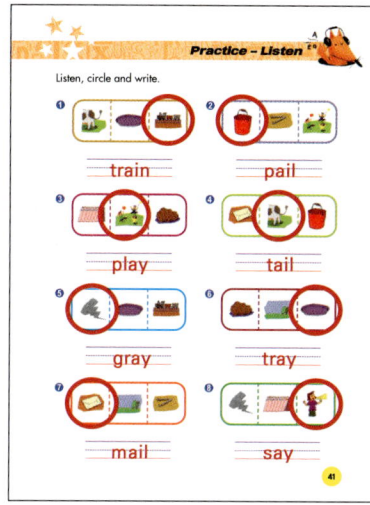

42p

❶ d
❷ a
❸ f
❹ b
❺ e
❻ c

43p

❶ ai / rain
❷ ai / nail
❸ ay / play
❹ ai / mail
❺ ai / train
❻ ay / day

Answer Key

44p
❶ tail
❷ gray
❸ rain
❹ pail
❺ play
❻ clay

play
pail
tail
rain pail
pail

48p
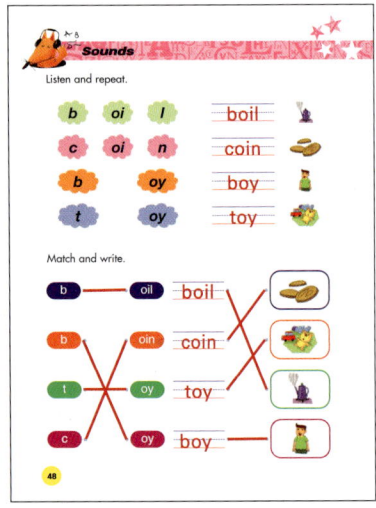

50p
oi
toilet
boil
soil
coin
oil
point

oy
toy
boy

51p

52p
❶ c
❷ f
❸ d
❹ a
❺ b
❻ e

53p
❶ oi / boil
❷ oi / coin
❸ oy / toy
❹ oi / join
❺ oi / oil
❻ oy / boy

54p
❶ coin
❷ soil
❸ join
❹ boy

soil
coin
coin
point coin
coin
join coin

Review1

56p

coin coat
boil pail
draw
seesaw
tail
toilet
Sheep
tree
pillow
snow
rain
road
play
gray
boil
coin
bowl
window
snow
straw
bean eat
say
toy
tea
sea
fault
feet
yawn yellow

57p
❶ coin   ❷ coat
❸ rain   ❹ tree
❺ seesaw ❻ soap

58p

59p

d a
b c

62p

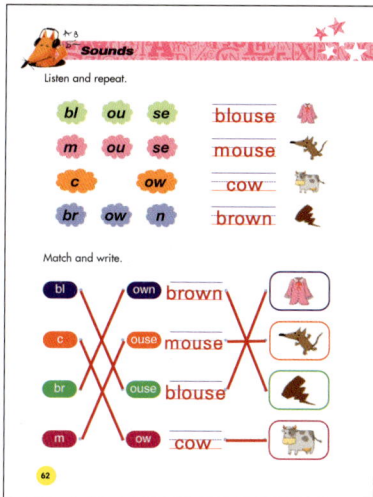

64p
ow
gown
owl
crown
clown

ou
count
blouse
house
mouse

65p

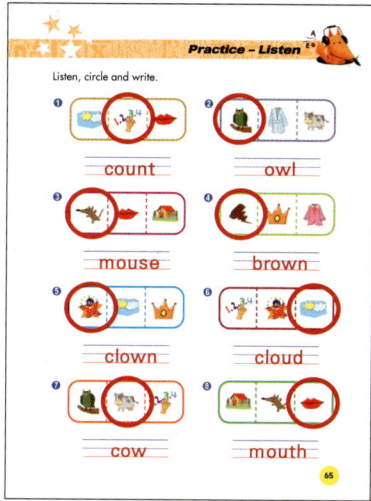

66p
❶ a
❷ f
❸ d
❹ c
❺ b
❻ e

67p
❶ ou / blouse
❷ ou / house
❸ ow / crown
❹ ow / owl
❺ ow / gown
❻ ou / count

Answer Key

68p
1. clown
2. gown
3. mouse
4. brown
5. mouth
6. count

clown
mouth
mouse
count
brown gown

72p
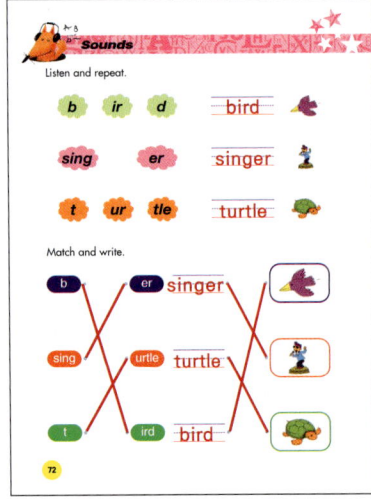

74p
ir
skirt
shirt
bird

er
teacher
soccer
singer

ur
nurse
purple
turtle

75p

76p
1. e
2. c
3. a
4. f
5. d
6. b

77p
1. ir / skirt
2. er / teacher
3. er / dinner
4. ur / nurse
5. er / soccer
6. er/ singer

78p
1. singer
2. nurse
3. bird
4. turtle
5. purple
6. girl

bird
singer
singer
purple nurse

82p

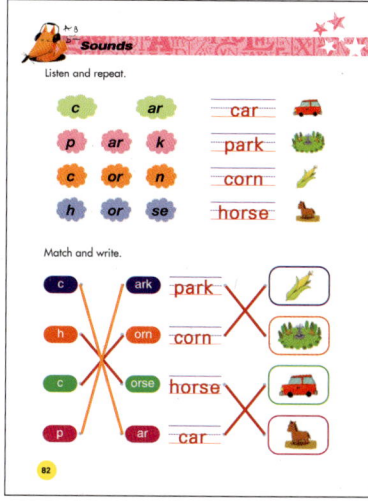

85p

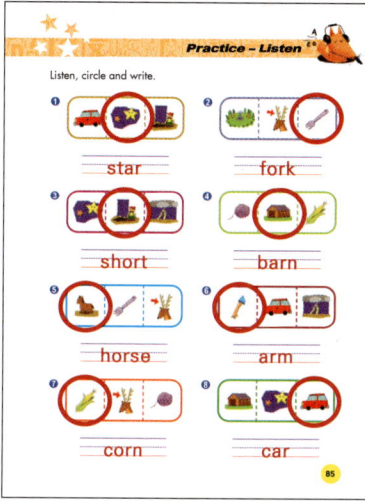

88p

❶ car
❷ star
❸ horn
❹ park
❺ horse
❻ corn

park
star
car
car
star
horse horn

84p

ar

arm
park
barn
car

or

corn
horse
short
fork

86p

❶ a
❷ c
❸ f
❹ b
❺ e
❻ d

87p

❶ ar / yarn
❷ or / storm
❸ ar / park
❹ ar / car
❺ or / corn
❻ ar / star

92p

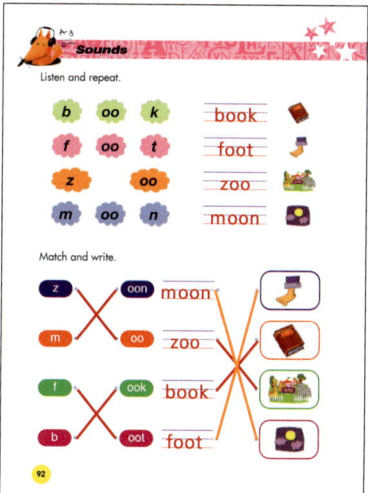

Answer Key

94p

oo[u]

cook
foot
look
wool

oo[u:]

boot
pool
goose
zoo

95p

96p

❶ e
❷ d
❸ b
❹ f
❺ a
❻ c

97p

❶ oo[u:] / zoo
❷ oo[u] / wood
❸ oo[u] / foot
❹ oo[u] / look
❺ oo[u] / book
❻ oo[u:] / boot

98p

❶ oo[u]
❷ oo[u:]
❸ oo[u:]
❹ oo[u:]
❺ oo[u:]
❻ oo[u:]

zoo
balloon
cook
pool
moon

100p

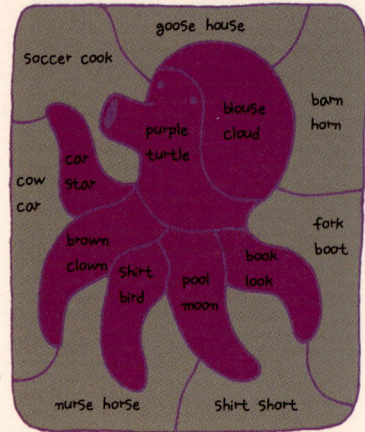

101p

❶ mouth
❷ mouse
❸ soccer
❹ wood
❺ corn
❻ clown
❼ bird

102p

120

103p

b	c
d	a

104, 105p

❶ c	❷ c	❸ a
❹ b	❺ c	❻ c
❼ a	❽ c	❾ b
❿ b	⓫ c	⓬ a

106, 107p

❶ point, singer
❷ yellow, blouse
❸ train, clay
❹ oil, coat
❺ turtle, short
❻ sausage
❼ mouse, balloon
❽ boy, soccer

108p

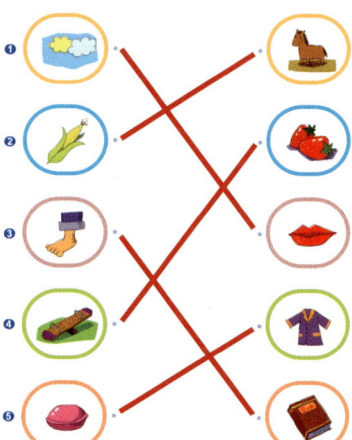

109p

❶ tree
❷ goat
❸ snow
❹ coin
❺ straw
❻ house
❼ fork
❽ moon

121

Answer Key

Activity

110p

111p

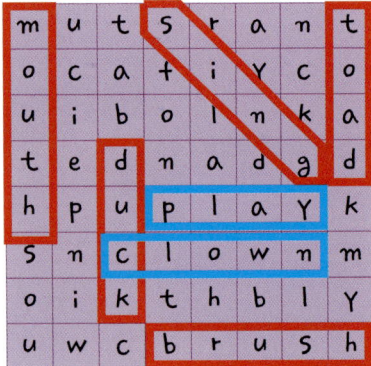

112p

❶ balloon

❷ crab

❸ count

❹ blue

❺ bowl

❻ girl

❼ brick

❽ king

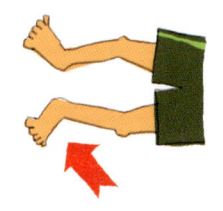

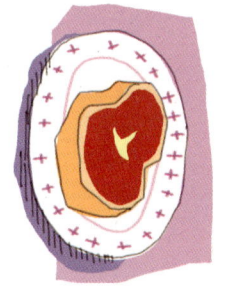

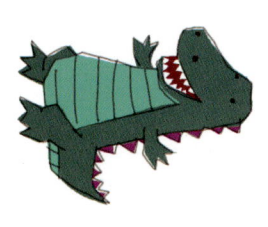

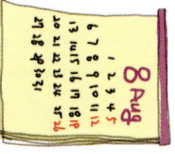

bee	feet	feed	sheep
sleep	tree	eat	sea
bean	meat	leaf	tea
August	autumn	fault	dinosaur

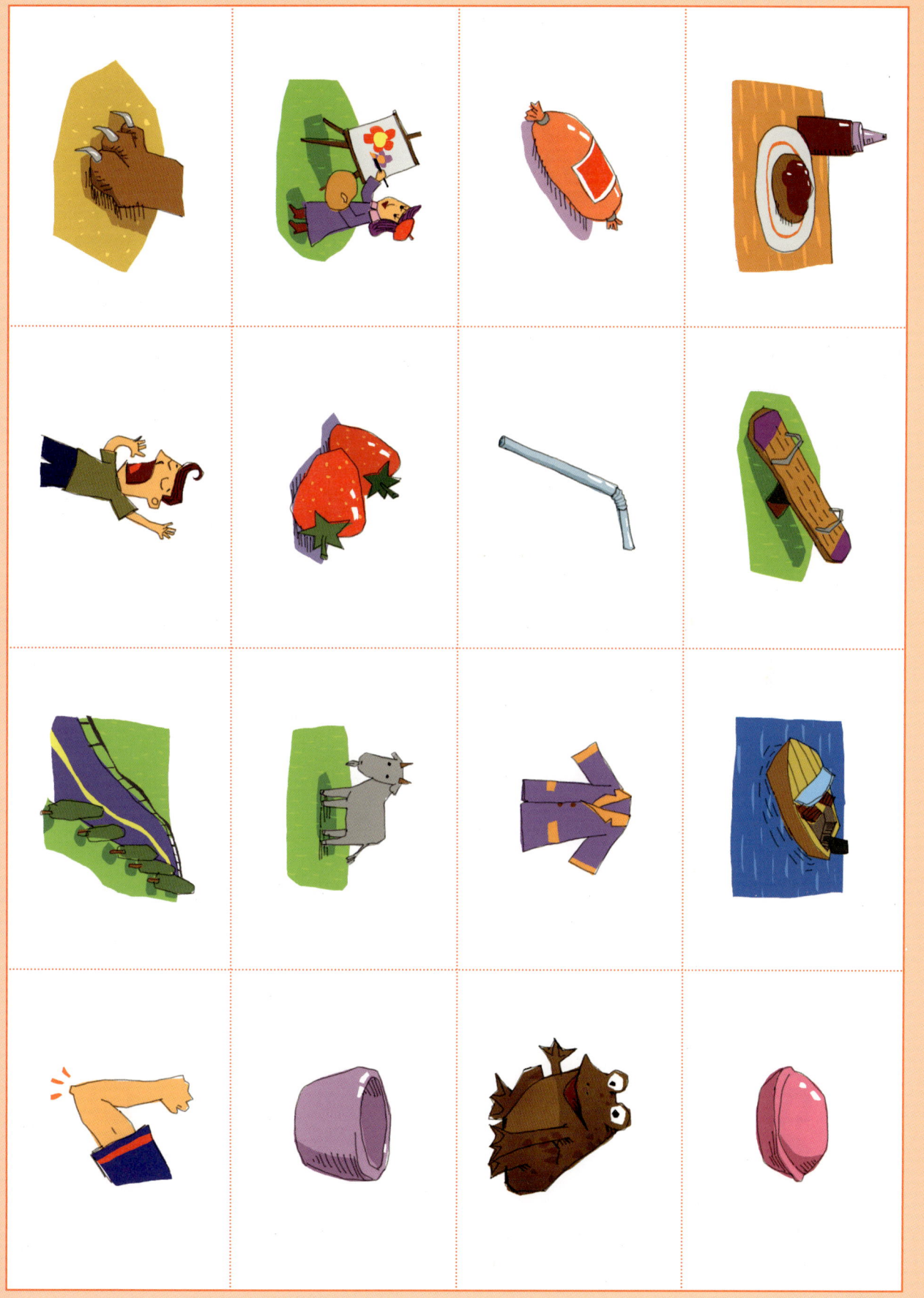

sauce

seesaw

boat

soap

sausage

straw

coat

toad

draw

strawberry

goat

bowl

paw

yawn

road

elbow

pillow	snow	window	yellow
mail	nail	pail	rain
tail	train	clay	day
gray	tray	play	say

cloud	toilet	join	oil
count	boy	noise	boil
blouse	joy	point	coin
house	toy	soil	foil

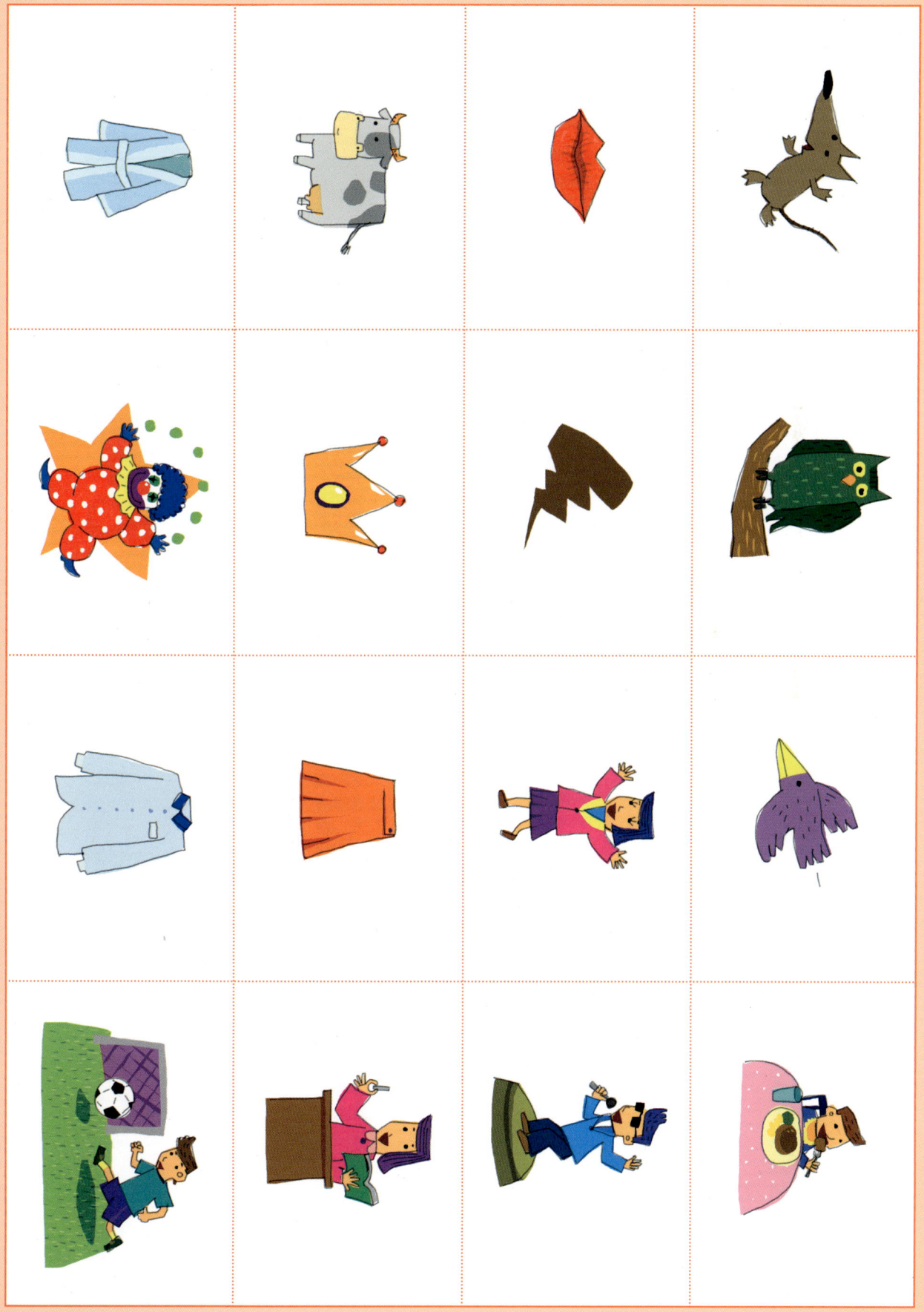

131

mouse	owl	bird	dinner
mouth	brown	girl	singer
cow	crown	skirt	teacher
gown	clown	shirt	soccer

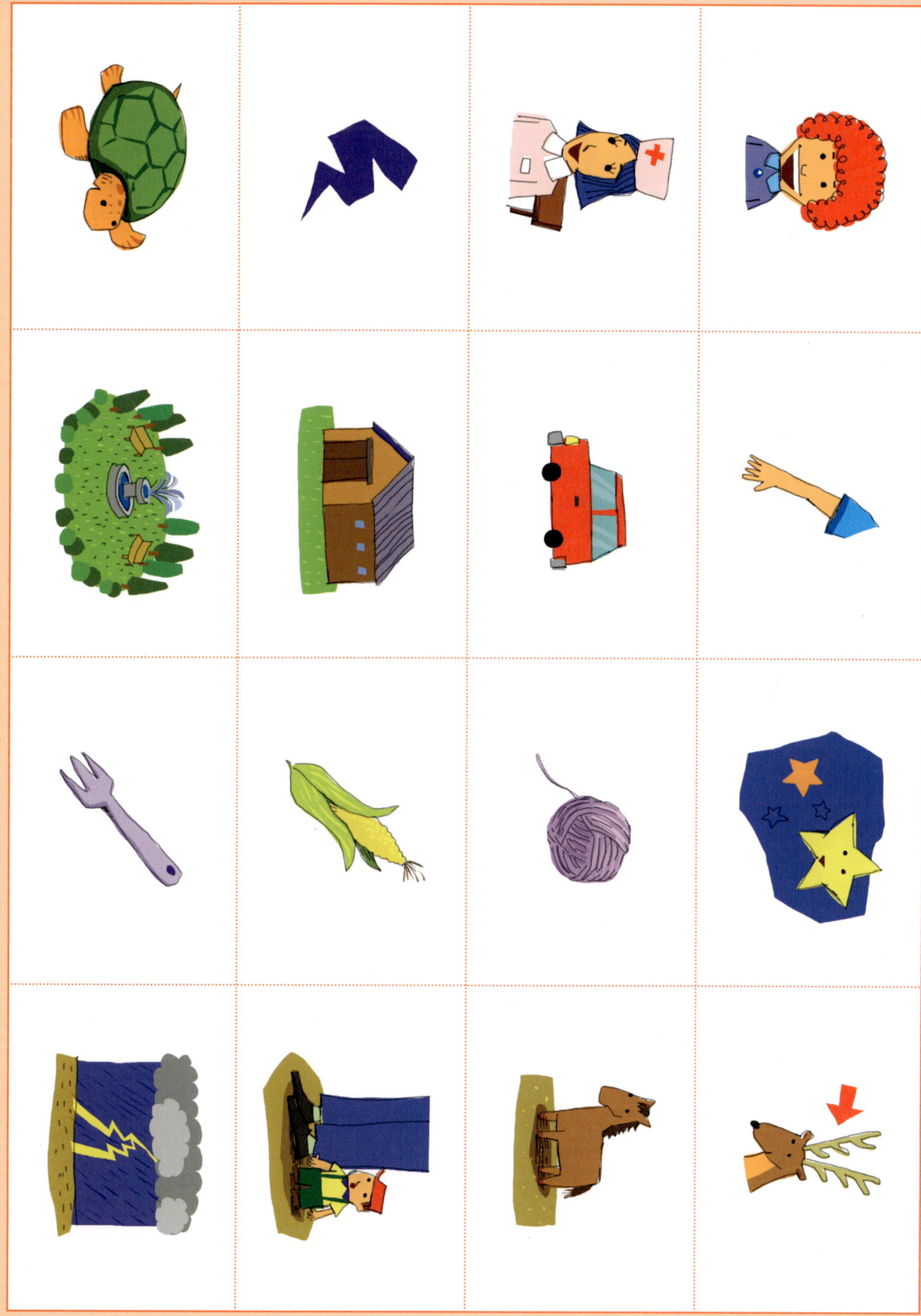

curl	nurse	purple	turtle
arm	car	barn	park
star	yarn	corn	fork
horn	horse	short	storm

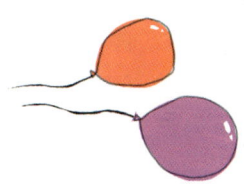

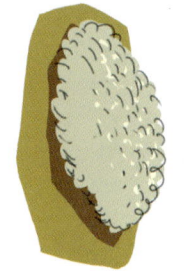

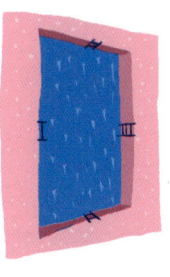

book	wood	pool
cook	wool	goose
foot	balloon	moon
look	boot	zoo

JUMP UP

Phonics

개정판 **4**

Double Letter Vowels ★ Workbook

ILR International Linguistics Research Institute

CONTENTS

Unit 1 Double letters ee ea

A Circle the correct picture for the same letters.

ee →

ea →

B Match the correct picture.

bean　　feet　　tea　　leaf

C Look and Check the correct words.

bee　bean

sea　tea

tree　leaf

sleep　sheep

D Check the pictures with the same letters.

E Do the puzzle.

F Read and Write the blank.

The _____ eats a leaf.

The kid _____s chicks.

The man _____s under the tree.

The monster has three _____.

The kid swims in the _____.

The bee drinks some _____.

G Look and Write.

bee

bee

Unit 2 Double letters au aw

A Circle the correct picture for the same letters.

au →

aw →

B Match the correct picture.

 seesaw 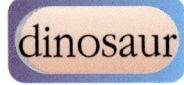 dinosaur 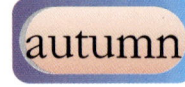 autumn 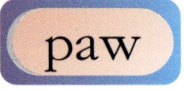 paw

C Look and Check the correct words.

☐ draw   ☐ straw

☐ sausage   ☐ sauce

☐ yawn   ☐ dinosaur

☐ paw   ☐ fault

D Check the pictures with the same letters.

E Do the puzzle.

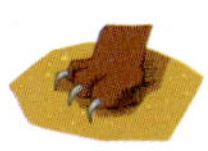

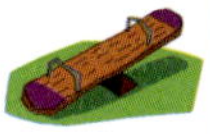

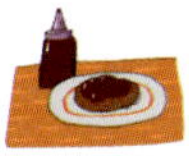

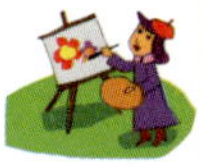

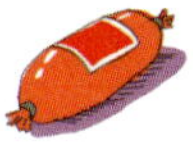

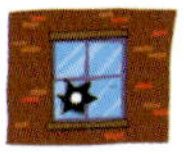

The man eats sausage with _____.

Dad _____s on the bed.

The frogs play on the _____.

The _____ sits on the stone.

The kid _____s a strawberry.

The bee drinks with a _____.

G Look and Write.

A Circle the correct picture for the same letters.

oa

ow

B Match the correct picture.

C Look and Check the correct words.

D Check the pictures with the same letters.

E Do the puzzle.

F Read and Write the blank.

A bee is in the _____ .

The _____ is in front of the window.

Mom washes the baby with _____ .

The kid has a _____ coat.

A _____ eats grass and leaves.

The truck is on the _____ .

G Look and Write.

A Circle the correct picture for the same letters.

ai →

ay →

B Match the correct picture.

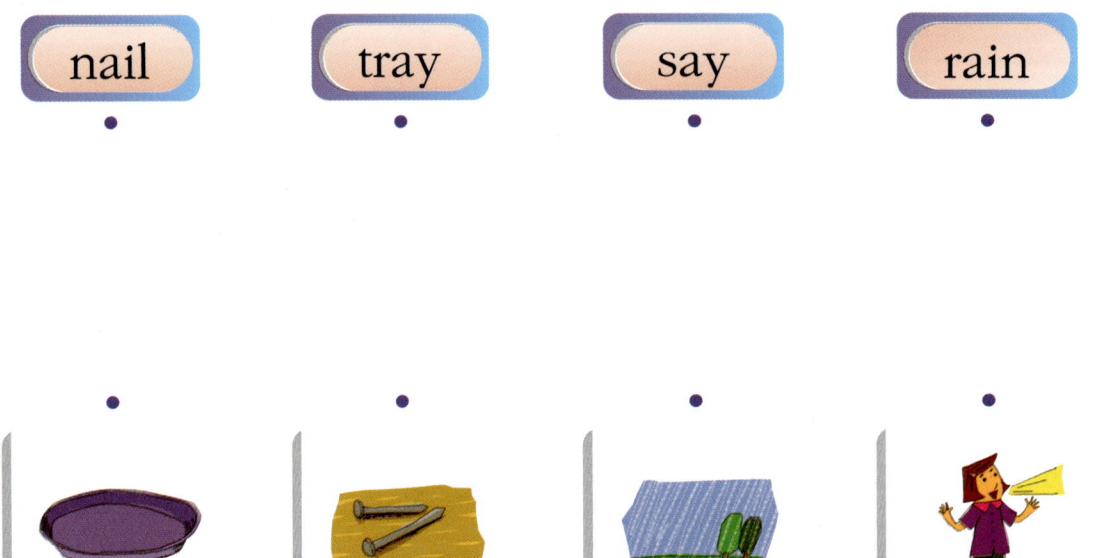

C Look and Check the correct words.

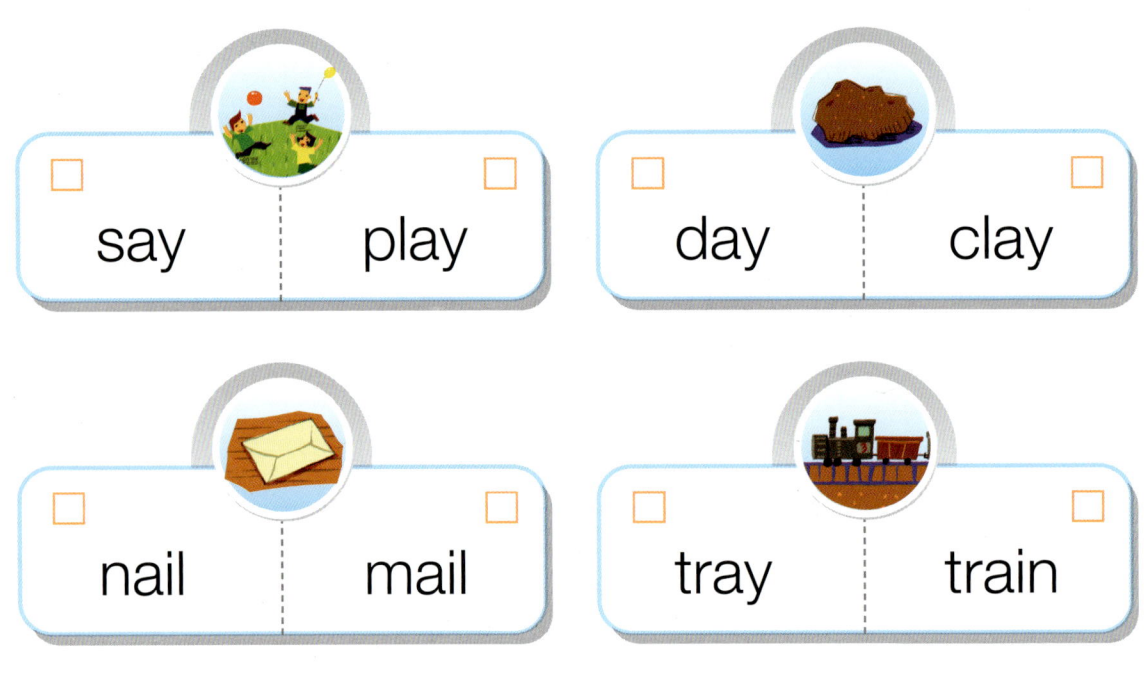

D Check the pictures with the same letters.

E Do the puzzle.

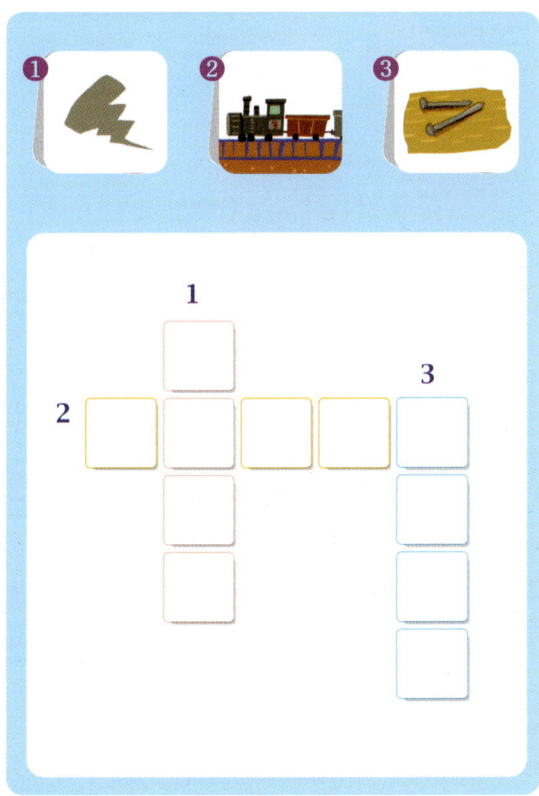

F Read and Write the blank.

The tree is in the _____.

There is a _____ on the boat.

The fox has a yellow _____.

The kid _____s with the top.

The man makes a _____ with clay.

The _____ nails are on the tray.

G Look and Write.

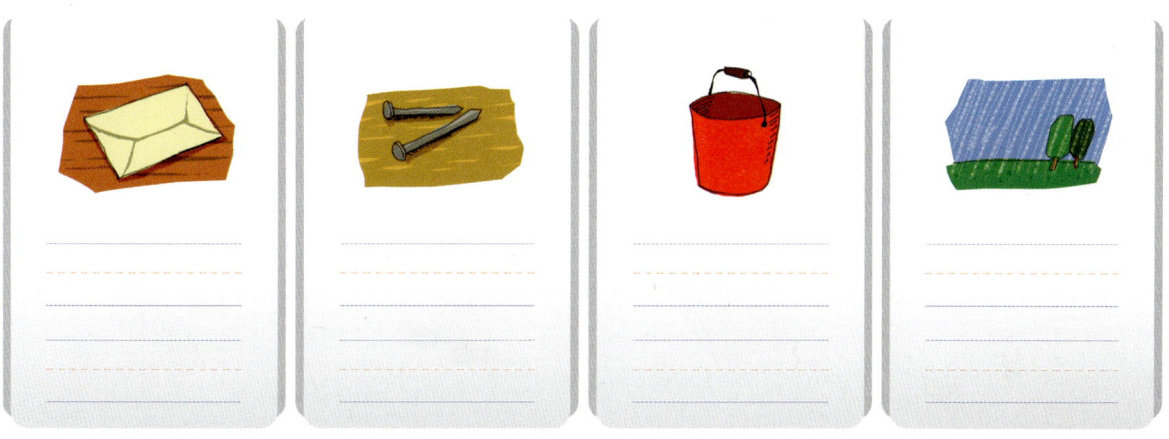

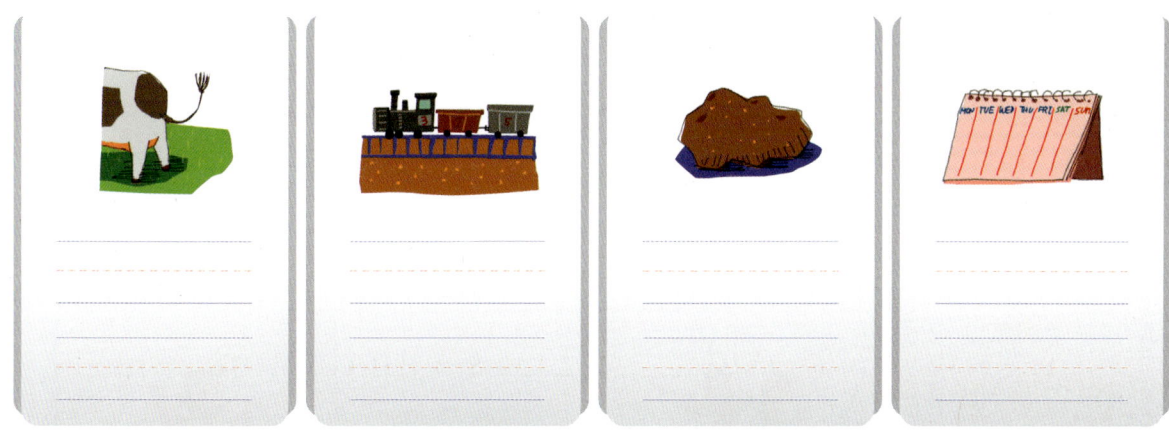

Unit 5 Double letters oi oy

A Circle the correct picture for the same letters.

oi

oy

B Match the correct picture.

| noise | toilet | foil | join |

C Look and Check the correct words.

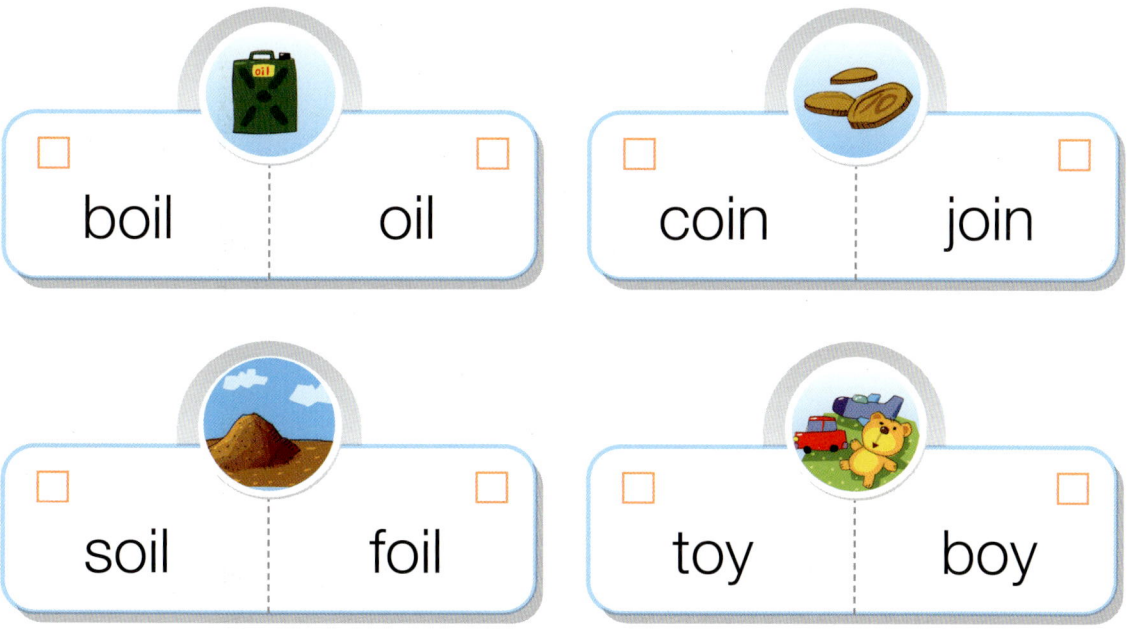

boil   oil

coin   join

soil   foil

toy   boy

D Check the pictures with the same letters.

E Do the puzzle.

F Read and Write the blank.

The dog puts the bone in the _____.

Mom _____s the eggs.

The _____s are on the tray.

The boy plays with the _____.

The _____ is on the coat.

The man _____s to the boat.

G Look and Write.

A Check the right word for the picture.

○ toad	○ coin	○ foil	○ join
○ toy	○ eat	○ gray	○ joy
○ day	○ rain	○ train	○ nail
○ dinosaur	○ elbow	○ pillow	○ snow
○ fault	○ strawberry	○ toilet	○ draw
○ sleep	○ say	○ sheep	○ soil

B Look and Match.

 aw   •   •  • •

 au   •   •  • •

 ea   •   •  • •

 ee   •   •  • •

 oa   •   •  • •

 ow   •   •  • •

ai   •   •  • •

C Choose and Write correct letters.

a	s	d	l	m	e	a	t	b	i	y	p
s	t	r	a	w	b	e	r	r	y	j	b
w	c	w	g	i	s	n	b	h	a	s	e
k	s	m	u	n	b	e	t	y	w	i	a
s	r	n	v	d	b	y	e	q	n	d	n
e	s	x	o	o	f	o	b	s	q	r	o
a	n	f	p	w	z	h	a	j	a	a	v
w	e	n	o	i	s	e	k	t	n	w	m

① snow

②

③

④

⑤

⑥

⑦

⑧

⑨

⑩

⑪

⑫

D Check the right letters.

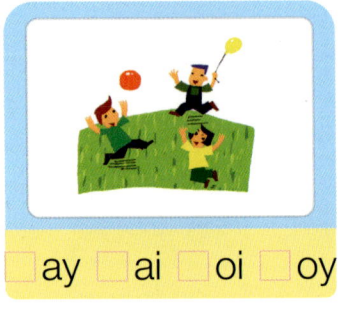
☐ ay ☐ ai ☐ oi ☐ oy

☐ au ☐ oa ☐ aw ☐ ow

☐ oi ☐ oy ☐ ay ☐ ai

☐ ee ☐ ea ☐ au ☐ ai

☐ aw ☐ ow ☐ au ☐ oa

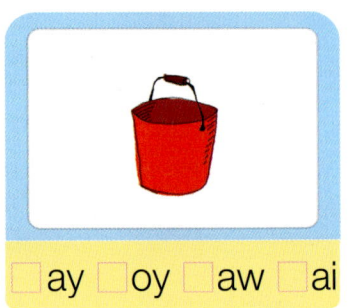
☐ ay ☐ oy ☐ aw ☐ ai

E Match the right picture.

 leaf

 window

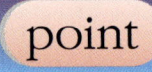 point

 sleep

F Write the missing letters.

n_____

c_____

s_____

g_____

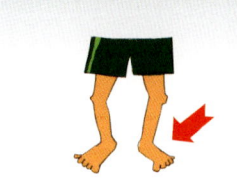

f_____

s_____

b_____

t_____

b_____

j_____

c_____

t_____

p_____

A_____

t_____

r_____

A Circle the correct picture for the same letters.

ou →

ow →

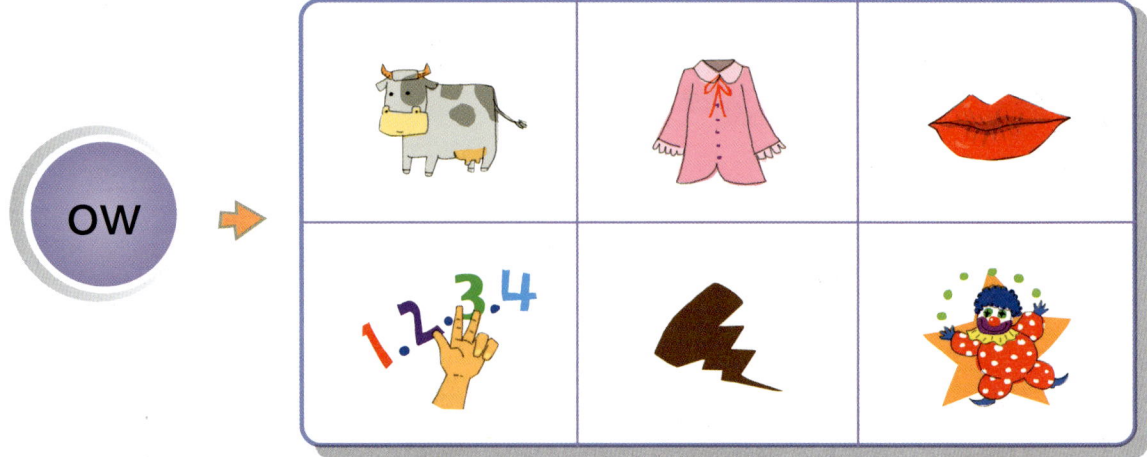

B Match the correct picture.

mouth	count	clown	cow

C Look and Check the correct words.

☐ blouse	☐ house

☐ clown	☐ crown

☐ brown	☐ gown

☐ mouth	☐ mouse

D Check the pictures with the same letters.

E Do the puzzle.

F Read and Write the blank.

The mouse _____ s the cats.

The dog has a _____ house.

Mom has a yellow _____.

The clown has a big _____.

The cow has a _____.

The _____ is on the tree.

Look and Write.

A Circle the correct picture for the same letters.

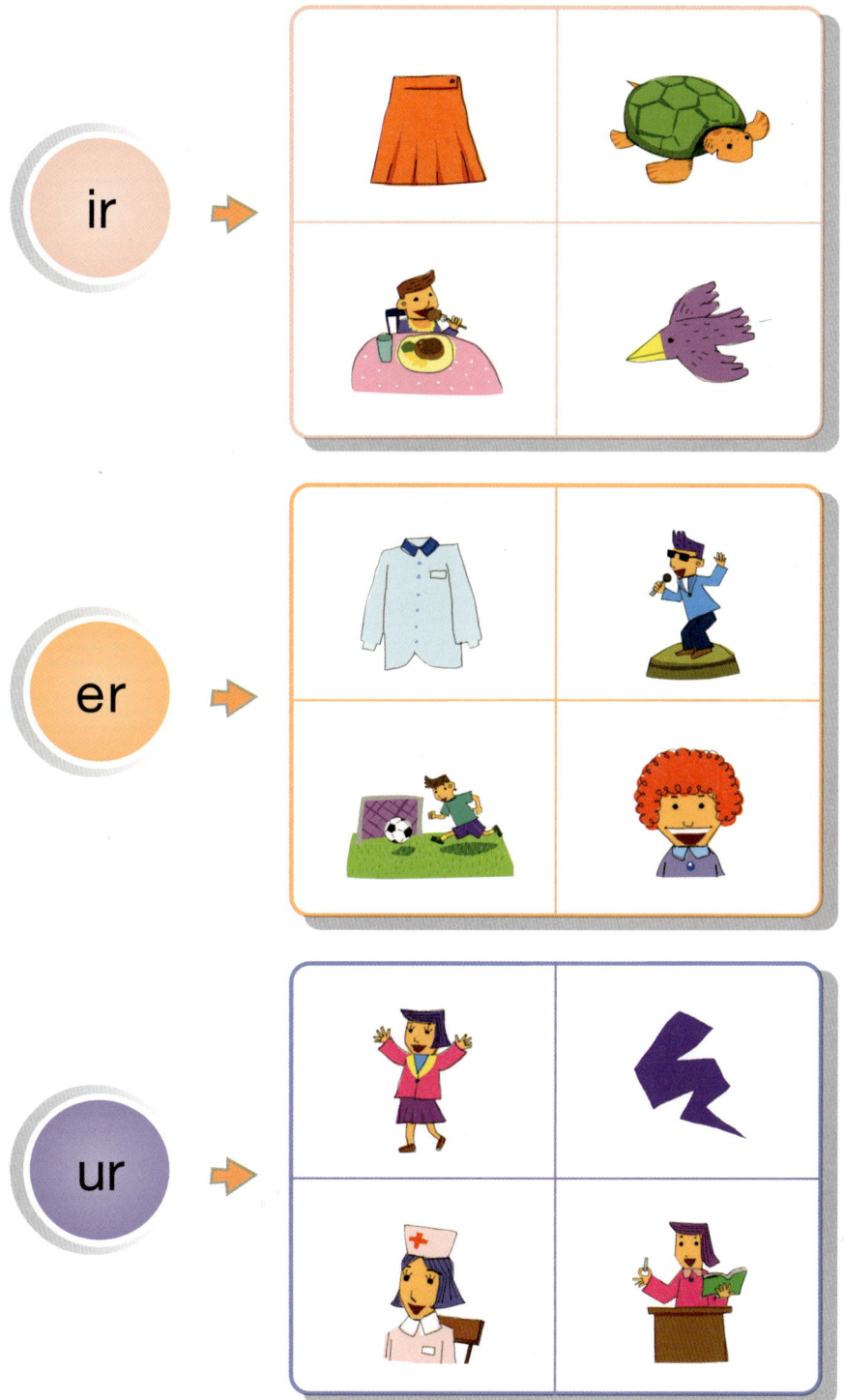

B Match the correct picture.

teacher   nurse   shirt   soccer

C Look and Check the correct words.

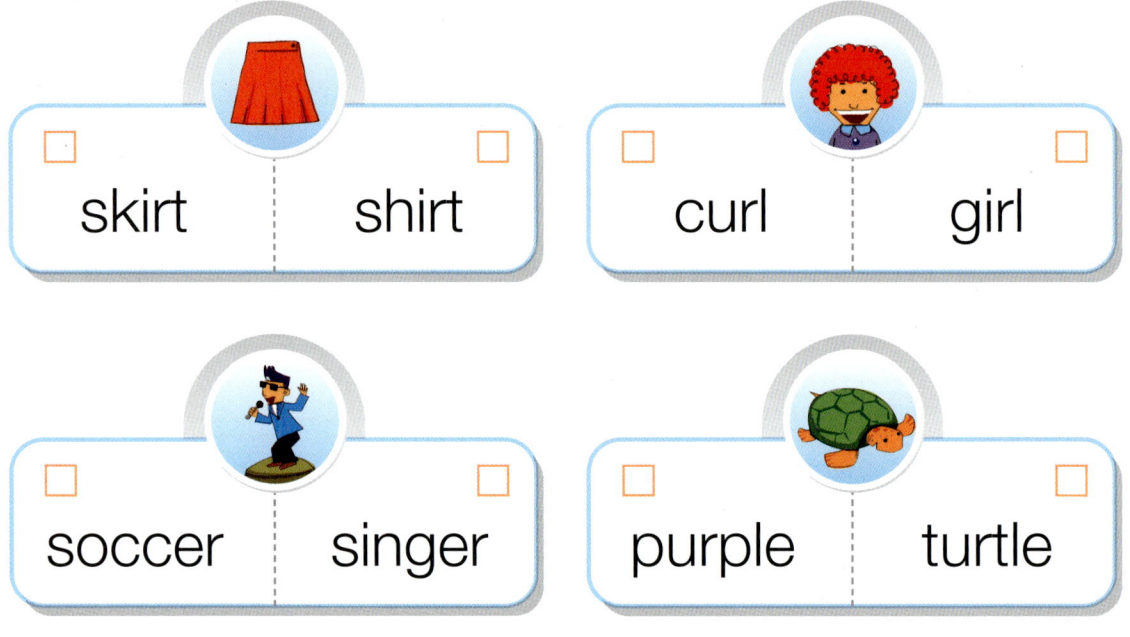

☐ skirt   ☐ shirt   ☐ curl   ☐ girl

☐ soccer   ☐ singer   ☐ purple   ☐ turtle

D Check the pictures with the same letters.

E Do the puzzle.

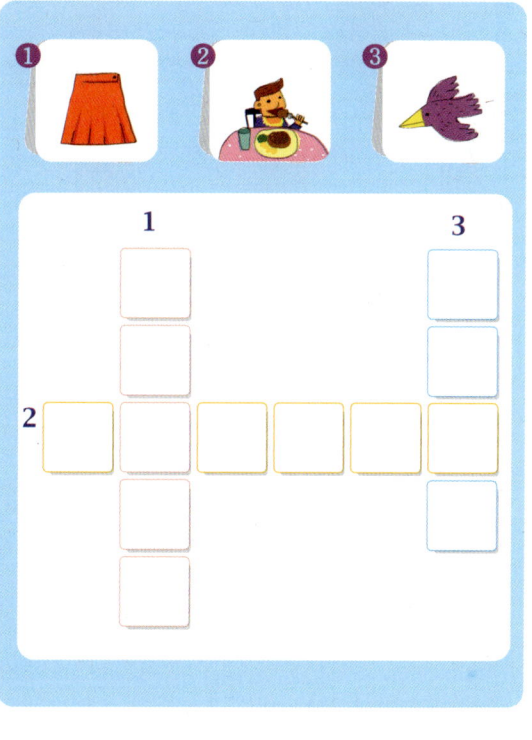

F Read and Write the blank.

The boy plays _____.

The _____ drinks some tea.

The _____ is on the tree.

The _____ counts the coins.

The _____ with curls has a yellow skir

The kid points to the _____ .

G Look and Write.

A Circle the correct picture for the same letters.

B Match the correct picture.

storm •   short •   yarn •   horn •

C Look and Check the correct words.

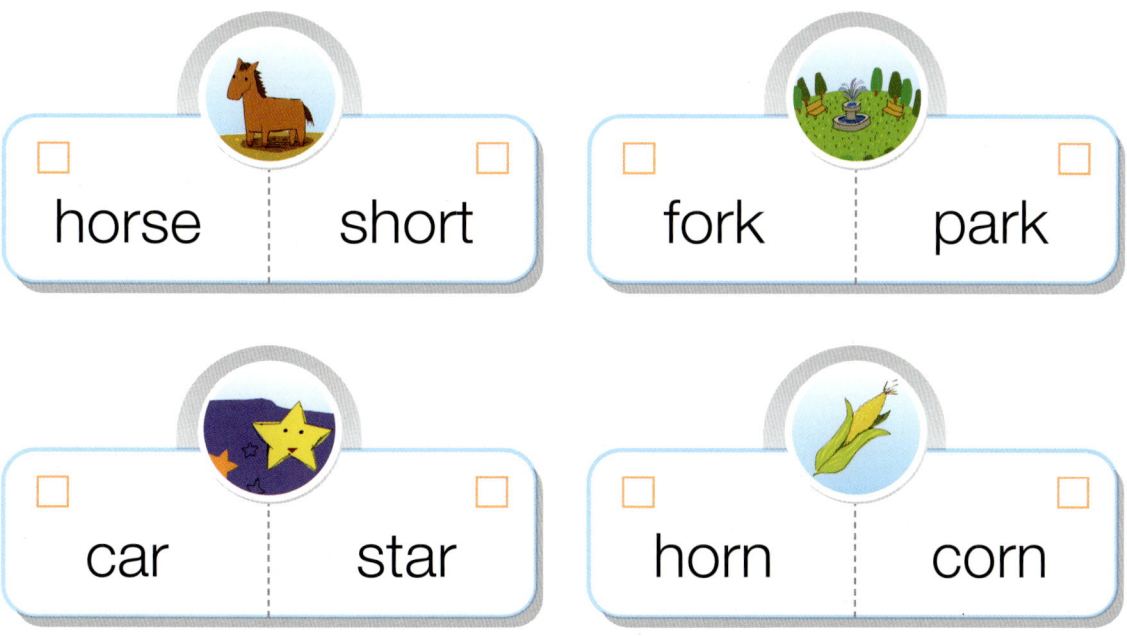

☐ horse   ☐ short

☐ fork   ☐ park

☐ car   ☐ star

☐ horn   ☐ corn

D Check the pictures with the same letters.

E Do the puzzle.

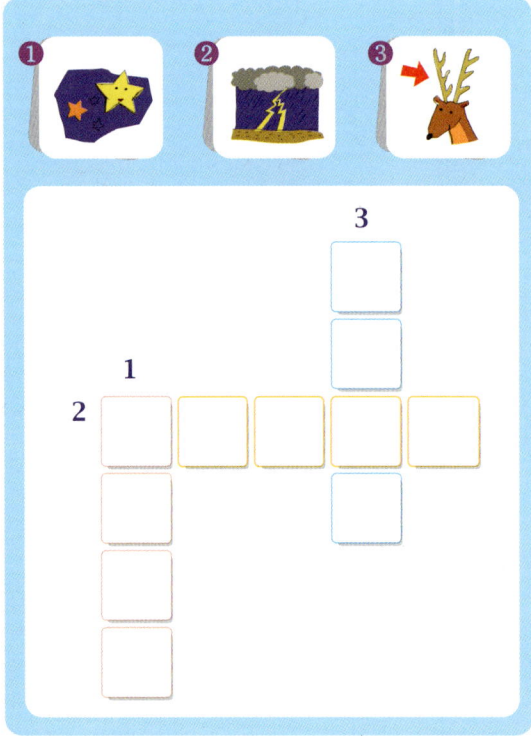

F Read and Write the blank.

The girl has dinner with a _____.

The turtle has a _____ neck.

The goat has _____s.

Mom has two _____s.

The horse is by the _____.

The boy likes the toy _____.

Look and Write.

A Circle the correct picture for the same sound.

OO
[u]

OO
[u:]

B Match the correct picture.

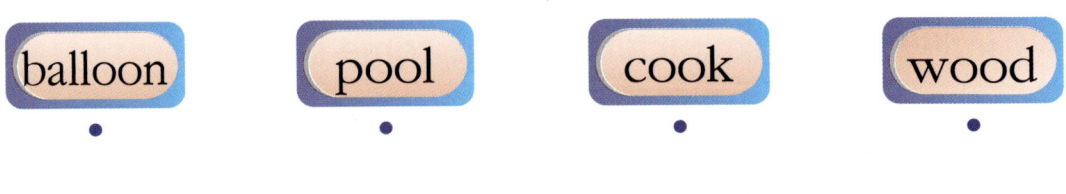

balloon   pool   cook   wood

C Look and Check the correct words.

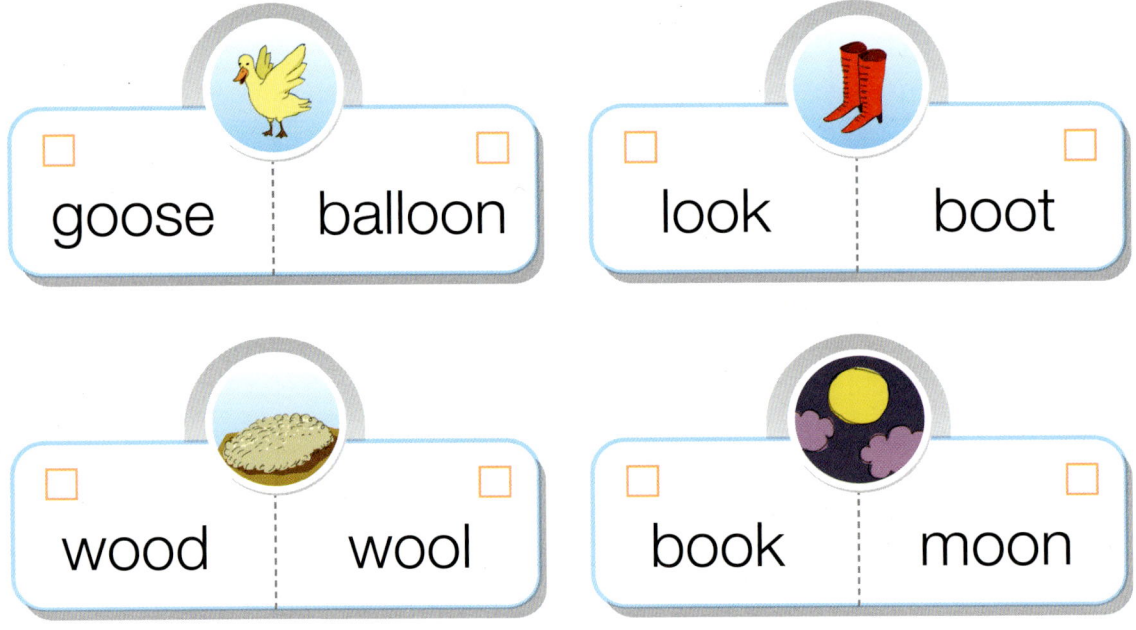

☐ goose ☐ balloon

☐ look   ☐ boot

☐ wood   ☐ wool

☐ book   ☐ moon

D Check the pictures with the same sound.

E Do the puzzle.

F Read and Write the blank.

The boy hurts his _____.

The mouse blows up the _____.

The turtle reads the _____.

The _____ looks at the moon.

The _____ makes strawberry pie.

The man makes a house with _____.

G Look and Write.

Review 2 Unit 6 ~ Unit 9

A Check the right word for the picture.

○ wool	○ pool	○ look	○ foot
○ horn	○ horse	○ house	○ cook
○ cloud	○ clown	○ crown	○ count
○ storm	○ short	○ shirt	○ skirt
○ wool	○ barn	○ wood	○ yarn
○ moon	○ nurse	○ mouth	○ mouse

B Look and Match.

C Choose and Write correct letters.

g	b	a	q	u	g	l	c	b	c	e	n
z	p	d	b	o	z	i	k	l	m	t	k
s	t	e	a	c	h	e	r	w	o	v	p
b	m	f	l	p	a	r	k	l	u	w	s
w	p	b	l	o	u	s	e	o	t	o	n
z	s	t	o	r	m	i	v	z	h	o	m
t	o	g	o	o	g	p	u	r	p	l	e
b	c	o	n	j	t	r	o	h	m	x	y

①  ②  ③  ④

_____ _____ _____ _____

⑤  ⑥  ⑦  ⑧

_____ _____ _____ _____

⑨  ⑩  ⑪  ⑫

_____ _____ _____ _____

D Check the right letters.

☐ or ☐ oo ☐ ou ☐ ow

☐ or ☐ oo ☐ ou ☐ ow

☐ ir ☐ er ☐ ur ☐ ar

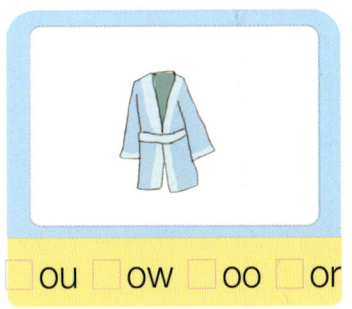

☐ ou ☐ ow ☐ oo ☐ or

☐ ar ☐ ir ☐ ur ☐ er

☐ oo ☐ ou ☐ ow ☐ or

E Match the right picture.

F Write the missing letters.

m_____

b_____

b_____

s_____

f_____

s_____

g_____

c_____

n_____

a_____

s_____

c_____

o_____

d_____

c_____

l_____

Final Test

A Check the correct picture.

B Write the missing letters.

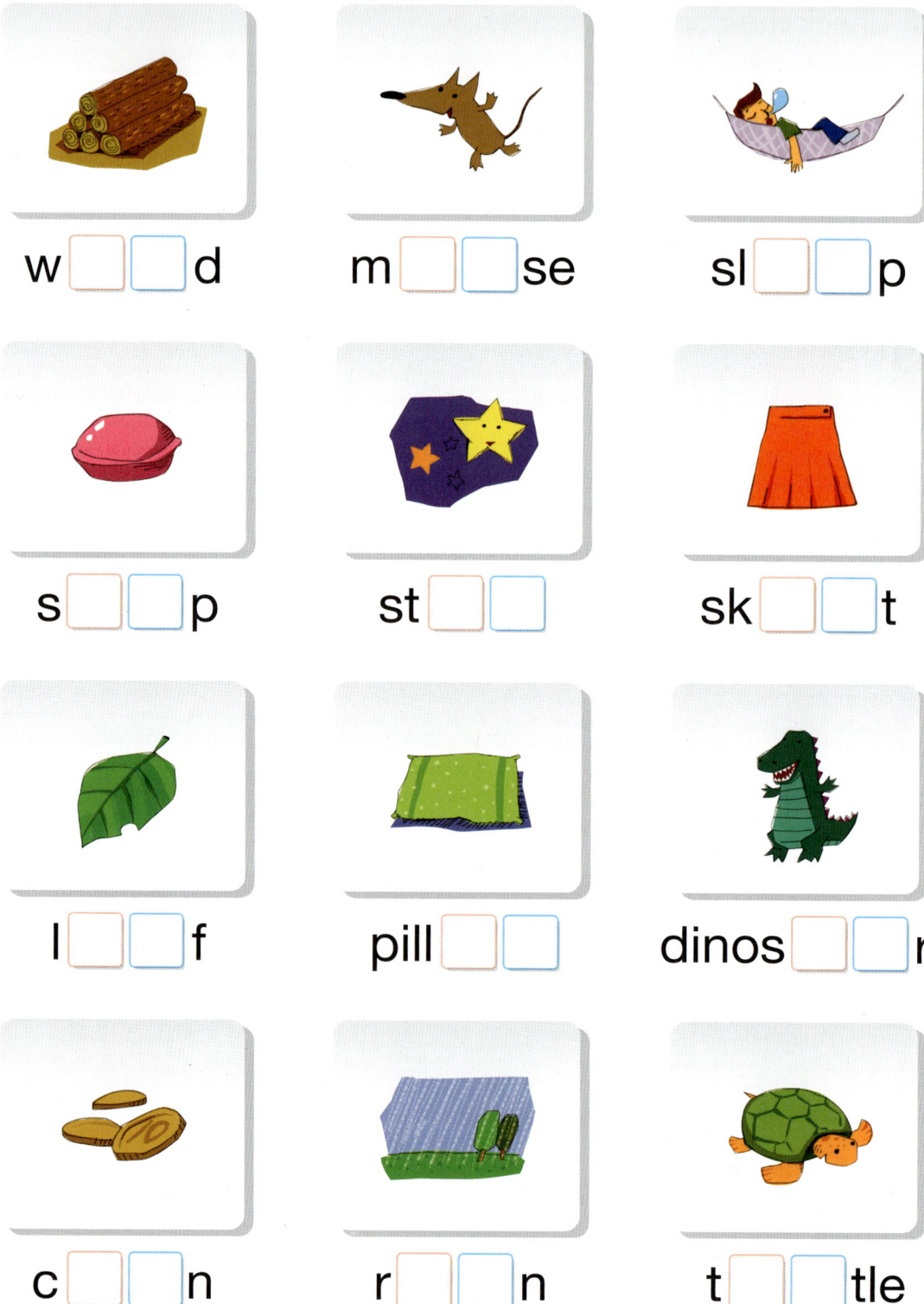

w ☐☐ d

m ☐☐ se

sl ☐☐ p

s ☐☐ p

st ☐☐

sk ☐☐ t

l ☐☐ f

pill ☐☐

dinos ☐☐ r

c ☐☐ n

r ☐☐ n

t ☐☐ tle

C Circle the correct pictures.

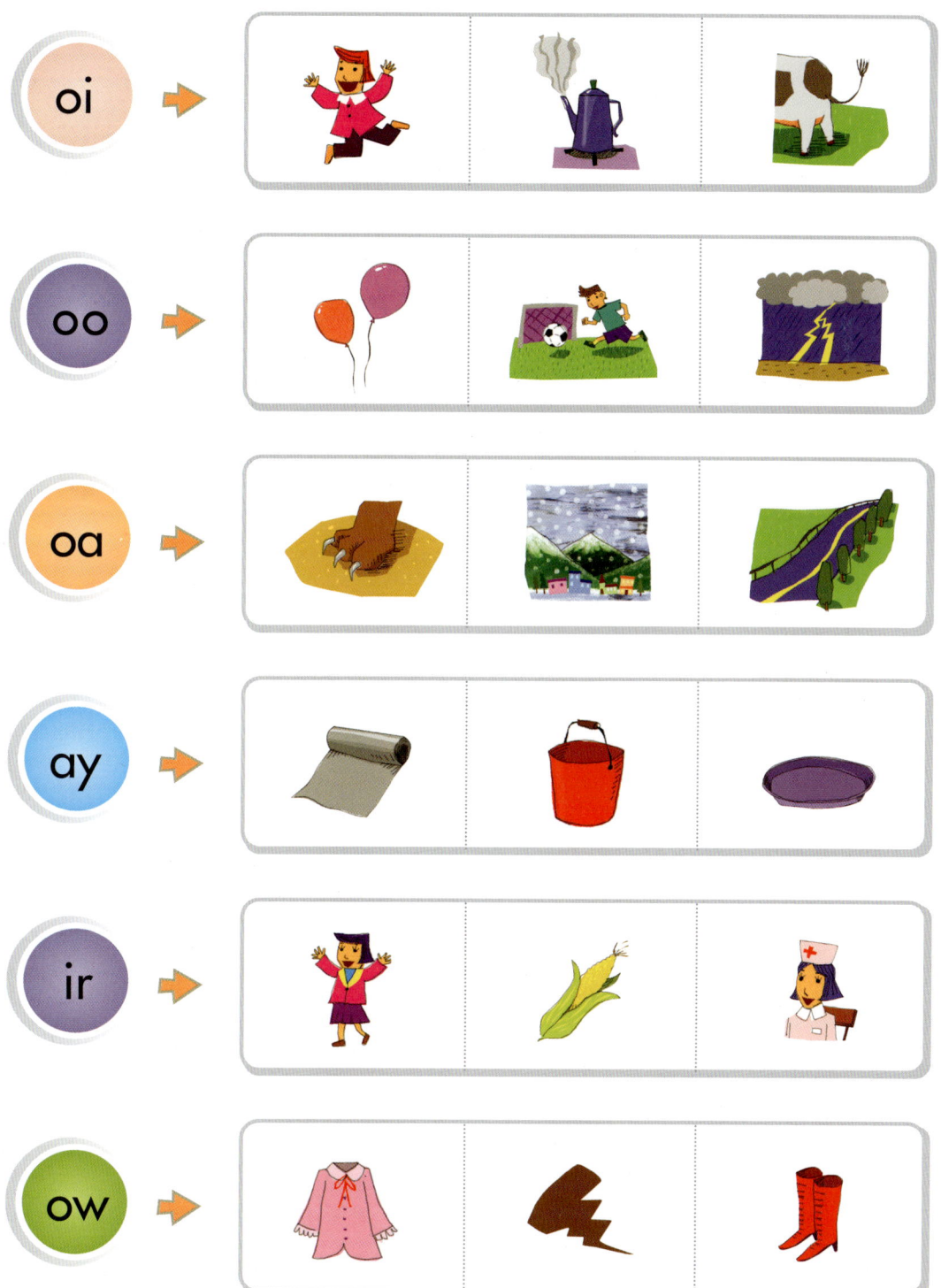

D Choose and Write correct letters.

or	ar	ou	ea	au	oa	oy	er	ur	oi	ow	oo

1 f [ ] [ ] t

2 s [ ] [ ]

3 d i n n [ ] [ ]

4 h [ ] [ ] s e

5 s [ ] [ ] s a g e

6 c [ ] [ ] l

7 y [ ] [ ] n

8 t [ ] [ ] d

9 p [ ] [ ] n t

10 c [ ] [ ] n t

11 b [ ] [ ]

12 e l b [ ] [ ]

E Write the correct words.

_____ _____ _____ _____

_____ _____ _____ _____

 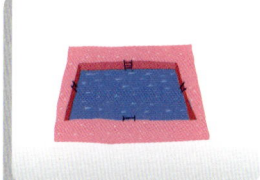  

_____ _____ _____ _____

 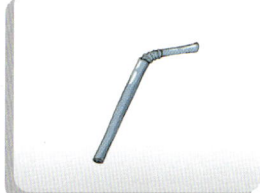  

_____ _____ _____ _____

Answer Key

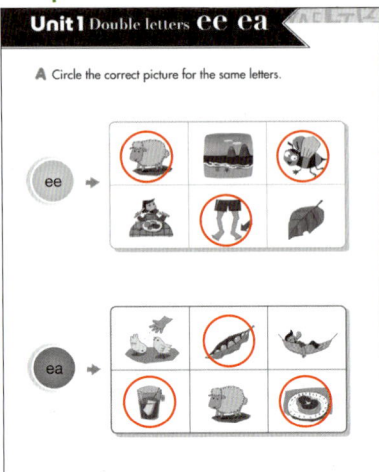

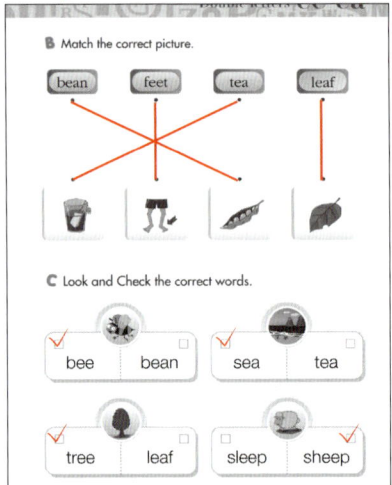

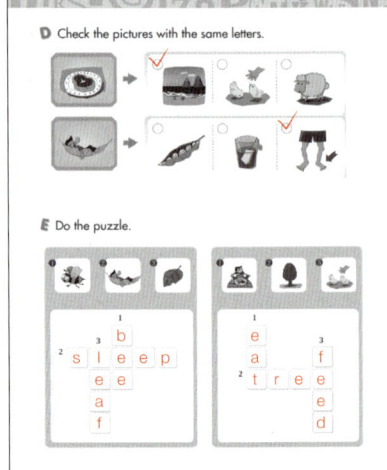

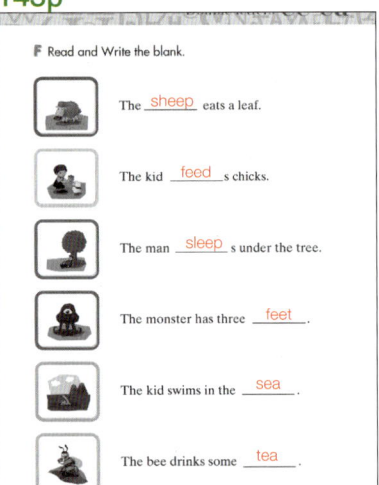

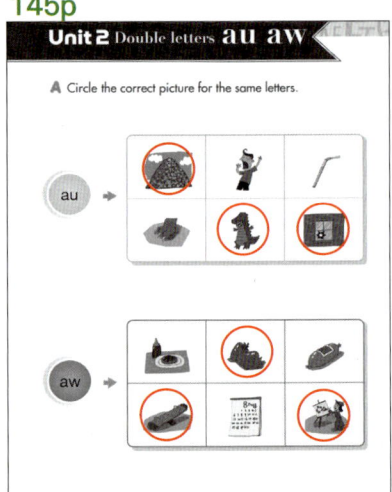

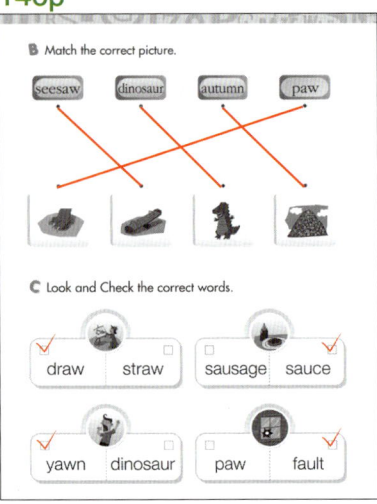

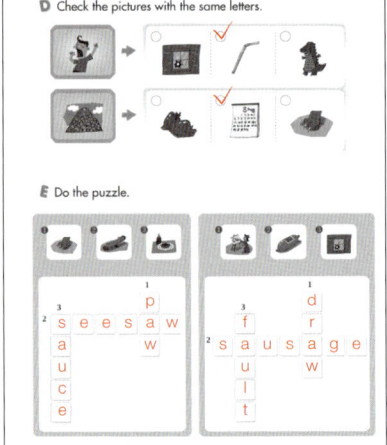

149p

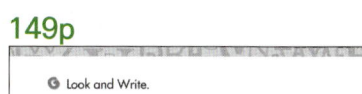

G Look and Write.

| August | autumn | fault | dinosaur |
| August | autumn | fault | dinosaur |

| sauce | sausage | draw | paw |
| sauce | sausage | draw | paw |

| seesaw | straw | strawberry | yawn |
| seesaw | straw | strawberry | yawn |

150p

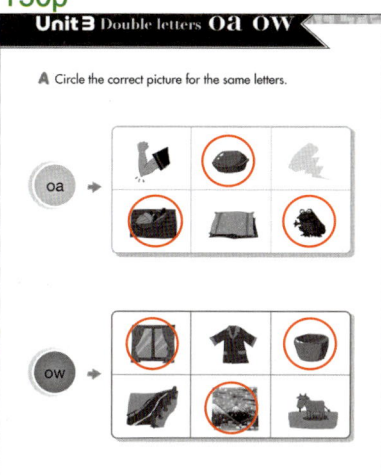

Unit 3 Double letters **oa ow**

A Circle the correct picture for the same letters.

oa →

ow →

151p

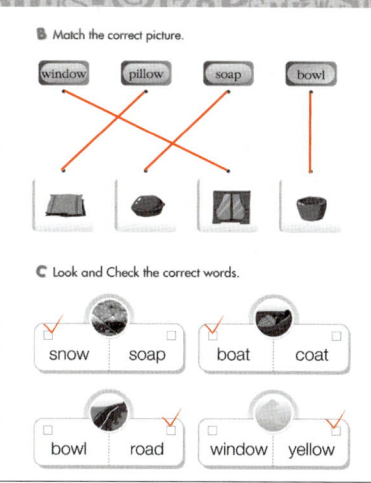

B Match the correct picture.

window   pillow   soap   bowl

C Look and Check the correct words.

snow / soap   boat / coat

bowl / road   window / yellow /

152p

D Check the pictures with the same letters.

E Do the puzzle.

```
        s           w
      3 n         3 i
2 e l b o w   1 c n
        o     2 t o a d
        a       a o
        t       t w
```

153p

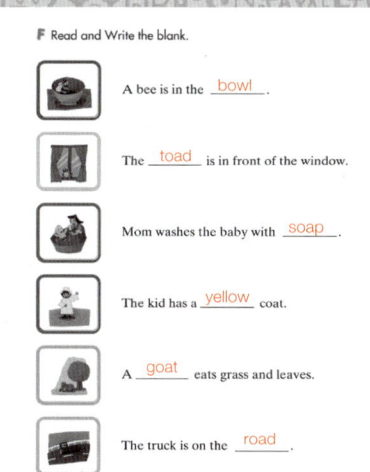

F Read and Write the blank.

A bee is in the   bowl .

The   toad   is in front of the window.

Mom washes the baby with   soap .

The kid has a   yellow   coat.

A   goat   eats grass and leaves.

The truck is on the   road .

154p

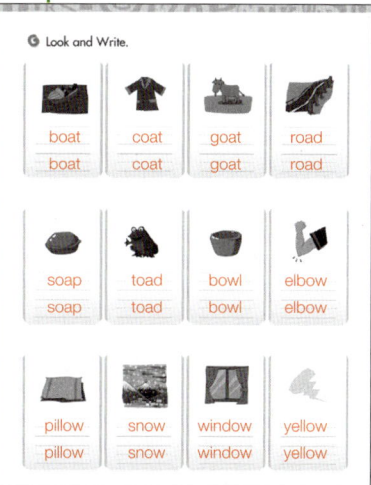

G Look and Write.

| boat | coat | goat | road |
| boat | coat | goat | road |

| soap | toad | bowl | elbow |
| soap | toad | bowl | elbow |

| pillow | snow | window | yellow |
| pillow | snow | window | yellow |

155p

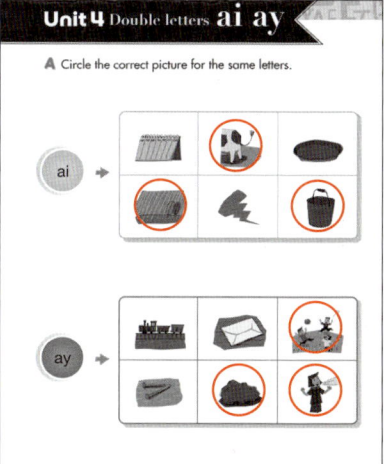

Unit 4 Double letters **ai ay**

A Circle the correct picture for the same letters.

ai →

ay →

156p

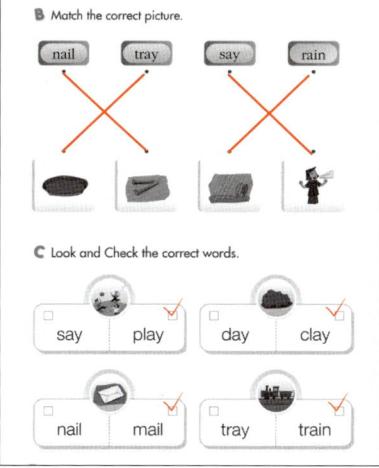

B Match the correct picture.

nail   tray   say   rain

C Look and Check the correct words.

say / play   day / clay /

nail / mail /   tray / train /

157p

D Check the pictures with the same letters.

E Do the puzzle.

```
      1 g       2 d
2 t r a i n     a
      a         1 y
      y     2 t r a y
                a
                l
                l
```

158p

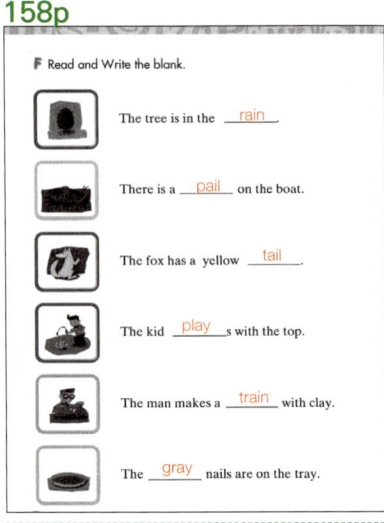

F Read and Write the blank.

The tree is in the ___rain___

There is a ___pail___ on the boat.

The fox has a yellow ___tail___.

The kid ___play___s with the top.

The man makes a ___train___ with clay.

The ___gray___ nails are on the tray.

159p

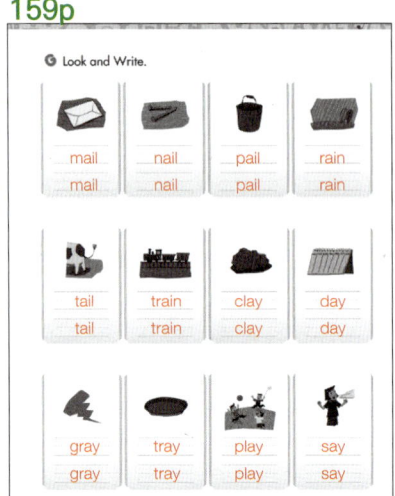

G Look and Write.

| mail | nail | pail | rain |
| mail | nail | pail | rain |

| tail | train | clay | day |
| tail | train | clay | day |

| gray | tray | play | say |
| gray | tray | play | say |

160p

Unit 5 Double letters oi oy

A Circle the correct picture for the same letters.

oi →

oy →

161p

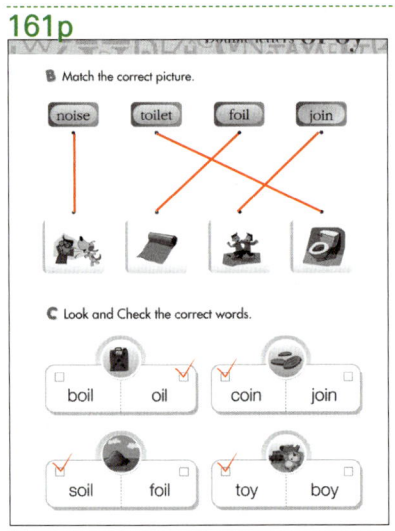

B Match the correct picture.

noise   toilet   foil   join

C Look and Check the correct words.

boil / oil   coin / join

soil / foil   toy / boy

162p

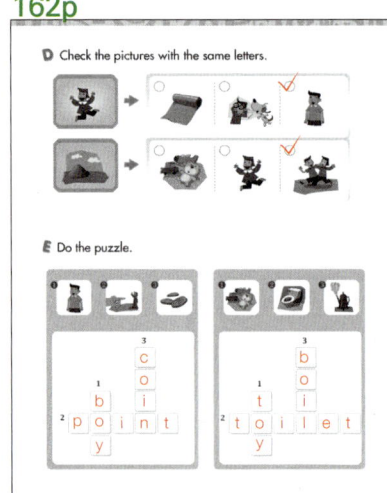

D Check the pictures with the same letters.

E Do the puzzle.

³ c o i
¹ b o i
² p o i n t
y

³ b o
¹ t o i
² t o i l e t
y

163p

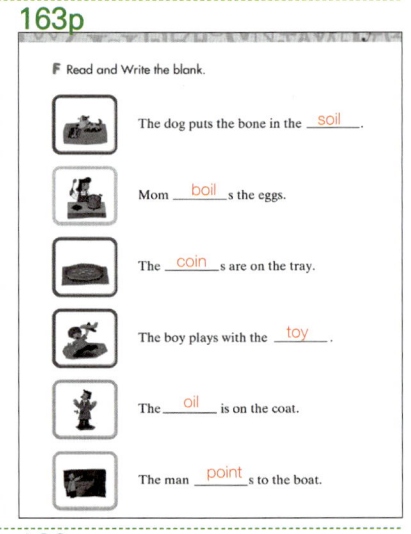

F Read and Write the blank.

The dog puts the bone in the ___soil___.

Mom ___boil___s the eggs.

The ___coin___s are on the tray.

The boy plays with the ___toy___.

The ___oil___ is on the coat.

The man ___point___s to the boat.

164p

G Look and Write.

| oil | boil | coin | foil |
| oil | boil | coin | foil |

| join | noise | point | soil |
| join | noise | point | soil |

| toilet | boy | joy | toy |
| toilet | boy | joy | toy |

165p

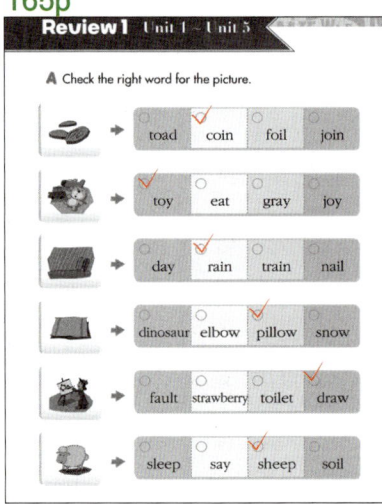

Review 1 Unit 1 ~ Unit 5

A Check the right word for the picture.

toad / **coin** / foil / join

toy / eat / gray / joy

day / **rain** / train / nail

dinosaur / **elbow** / pillow / snow

fault / strawberry / **toilet** / draw

sleep / say / **sheep** / soil

166p

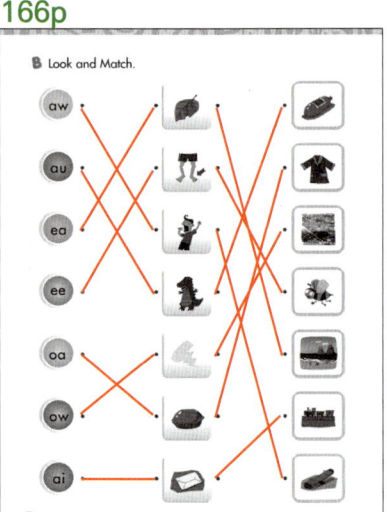

B Look and Match.

aw
au
ea
ee
oa
ow
ai

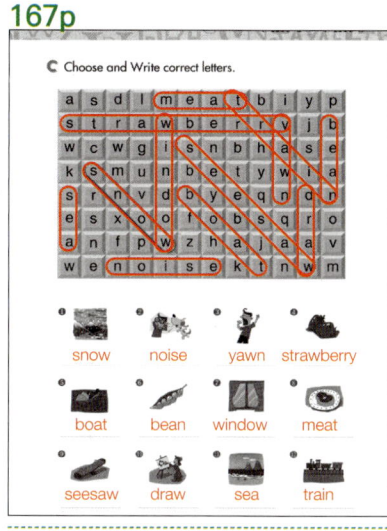

167p

C Choose and Write correct letters.

snow noise yawn strawberry

boat bean window meat

seesaw draw sea train

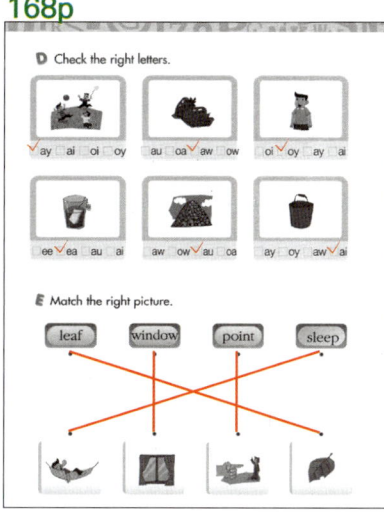

168p

D Check the right letters.

E Match the right picture.

leaf window point sleep

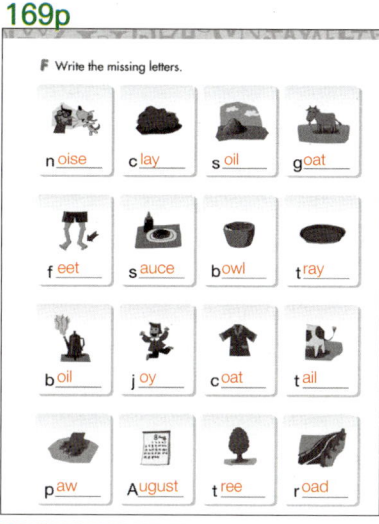

169p

F Write the missing letters.

n oise c lay s oil g oat

f eet s auce b owl t ray

b oil j oy c oat t ail

p aw A ugust t ree r oad

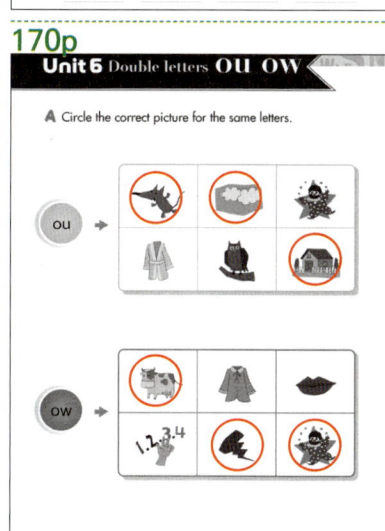

170p

Unit 6 Double letters OU OW

A Circle the correct picture for the same letters.

ou

ow

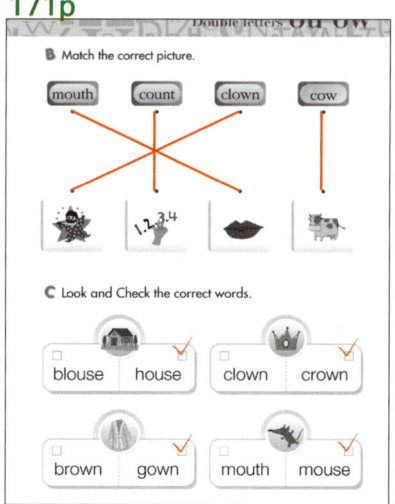

171p

Double letters OU OW

B Match the correct picture.

mouth count clown cow

C Look and Check the correct words.

blouse house clown crown

brown gown mouth mouse

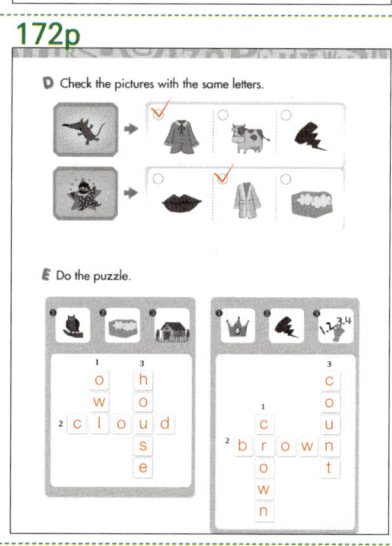

172p

D Check the pictures with the same letters.

E Do the puzzle.

1 o w l
2 c l o u d
3 h o u s e

1 c o u n t
2 b r o w n

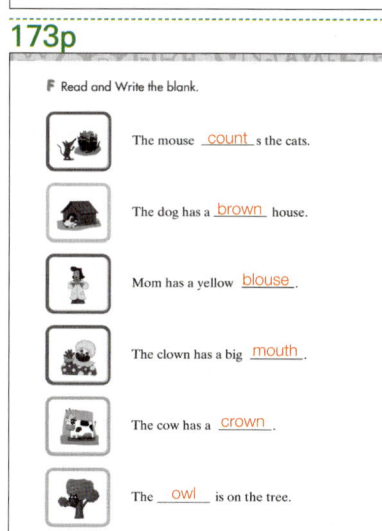

173p

F Read and Write the blank.

The mouse count s the cats.

The dog has a brown house.

Mom has a yellow blouse .

The clown has a big mouth .

The cow has a crown .

The owl is on the tree.

174p

G Look and Write.

cloud count blouse house
cloud count blouse house

mouse mouth cow gown
mouse mouth cow gown

owl brown crown clown
owl brown crown clown

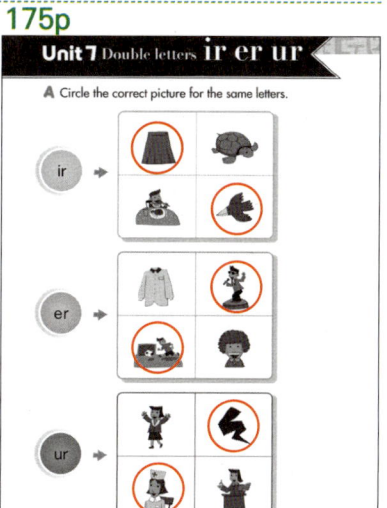

175p

Unit 7 Double letters ir er ur

A Circle the correct picture for the same letters.

ir

er

ur

Answer Key

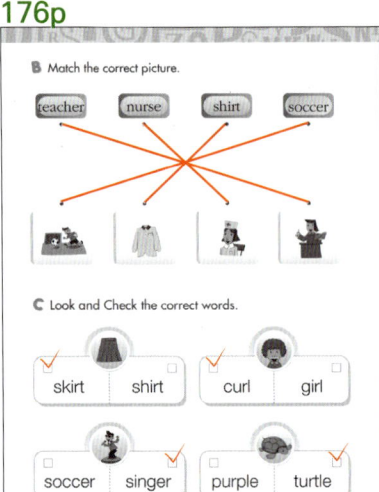

B Match the correct picture.

teacher   nurse   shirt   soccer

C Look and Check the correct words.

skirt ✓   shirt

curl ✓   girl

soccer   singer ✓

purple   turtle ✓

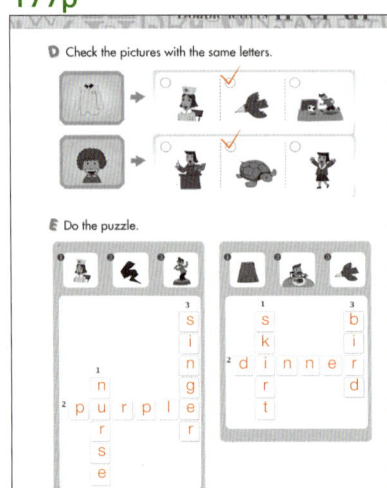

D Check the pictures with the same letters.

E Do the puzzle.

```
        s
        i
        n
  p u r p l e r
        s
        e
```

```
        1       3
        s       b
        k       i
  d i n n e r   r
        r       d
        t
```

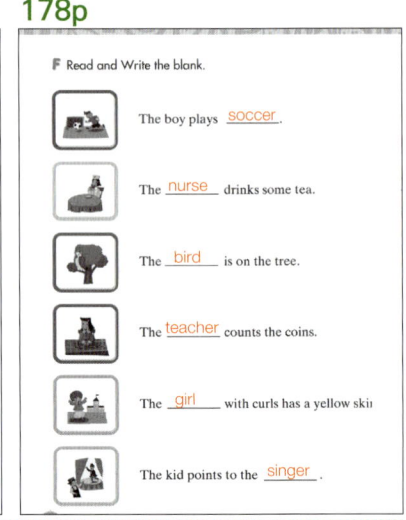

F Read and Write the blank.

The boy plays ___soccer___ .

The ___nurse___ drinks some tea.

The ___bird___ is on the tree.

The ___teacher___ counts the coins.

The ___girl___ with curls has a yellow skirt.

The kid points to the ___singer___ .

G Look and Write.

bird   girl   skirt   shirt
bird   girl   skirt   shirt

dinner   singer   teacher   soccer
dinner   singer   teacher   soccer

curl   nurse   purple   turtle
curl   nurse   purple   turtle

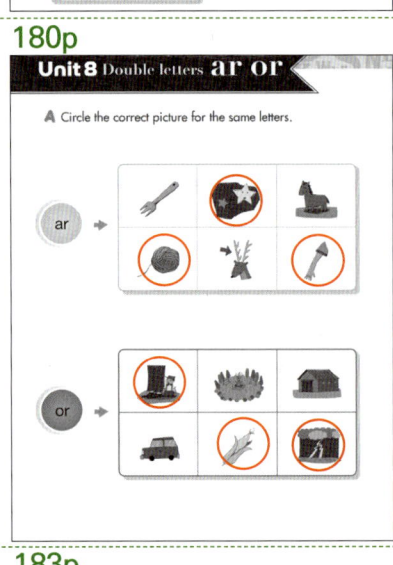

Unit 8 Double letters **ar or**

A Circle the correct picture for the same letters.

ar →

or →

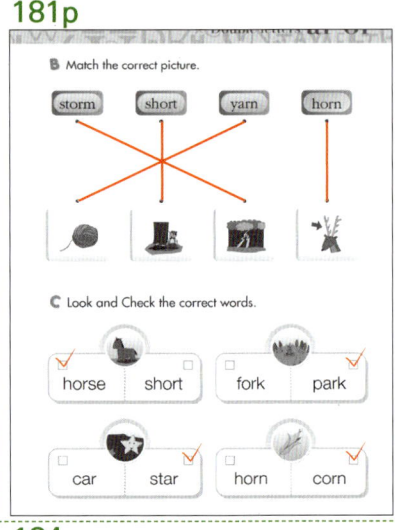

B Match the correct picture.

storm   short   yarn   horn

C Look and Check the correct words.

horse ✓   short

fork   park ✓

car   star

horn   corn ✓

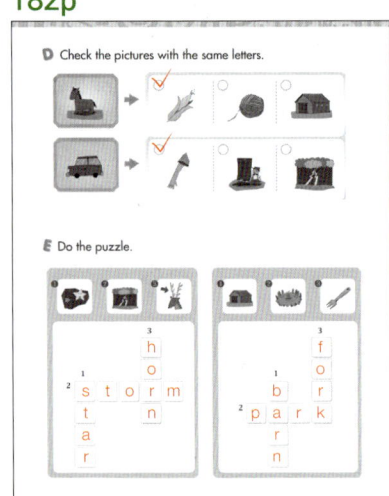

D Check the pictures with the same letters.

E Do the puzzle.

```
        3
        h
        o
  s t o r m
        t
        a
        r
```

```
        3
        f
        o
        r
  b     k
  p a r k
  r
  n
```

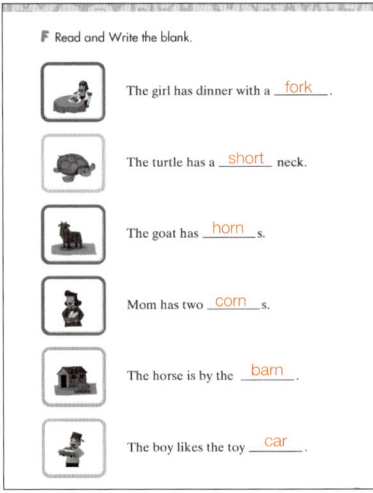

F Read and Write the blank.

The girl has dinner with a ___fork___ .

The turtle has a ___short___ neck.

The goat has ___horn___ s.

Mom has two ___corn___ s.

The horse is by the ___barn___ .

The boy likes the toy ___car___ .

G Look and Write.

arm   car   barn   park
arm   car   barn   park

star   yarn   corn   fork
star   yarn   corn   fork

horn   horse   short   storm
horn   horse   short   storm

Answer Key

185p

Unit 9 Double letters OO

A Circle the correct picture for the same sound.

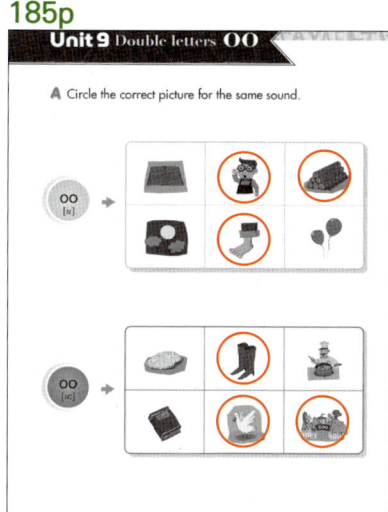

186p

B Match the correct picture.

C Look and Check the correct words.

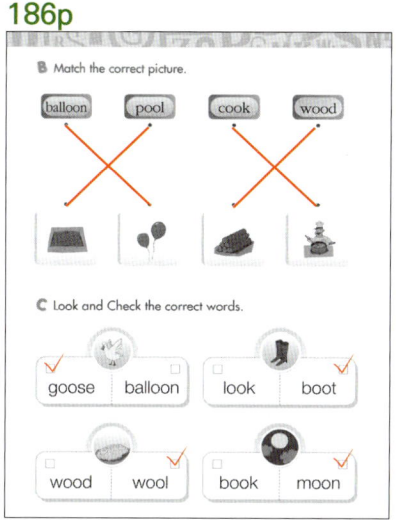

goose / balloon
look / boot
wood / wool
book / moon

187p

D Check the pictures with the same sound.

E Do the puzzle.

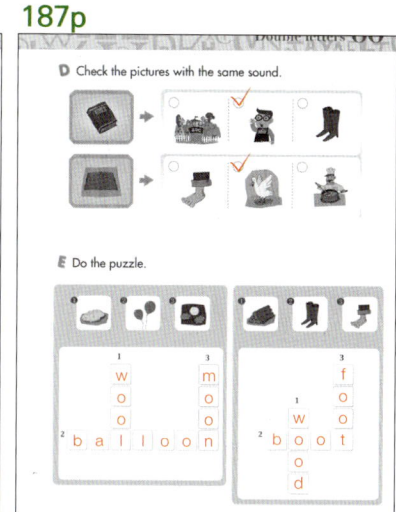

188p

F Read and Write the blank.

The boy hurts his __foot__.

The mouse blows up the __balloon__.

The turtle reads the __book__.

The __goose__ looks at the moon.

The __cook__ makes strawberry pie.

The man makes a house with __wood__.

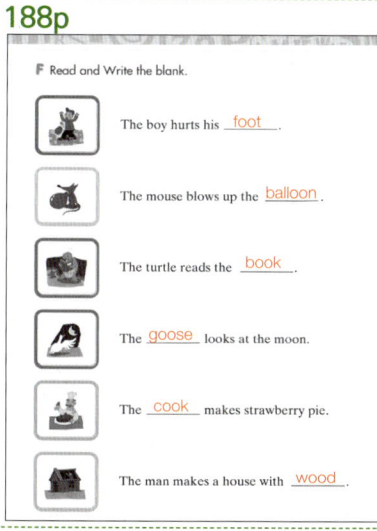

189p

G Look and Write.

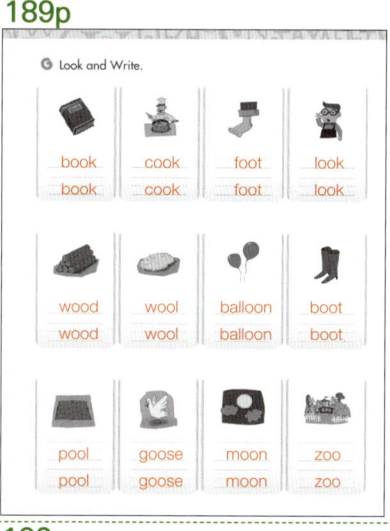

book / book
cook / cook
foot / foot
look / look

wood / wood
wool / wool
balloon / balloon
boot / boot

pool / pool
goose / goose
moon / moon
zoo / zoo

190p

Review 2 Unit 6 ~ Unit 9

A Check the right word for the picture.

wool / pool / look / foot
horn / horse / house / cook
cloud / clown / crown / count
storm / short / shirt / skirt
wool / barn / wood / yarn
moon / nurse / mouth / mouse

191p

B Look and Match.

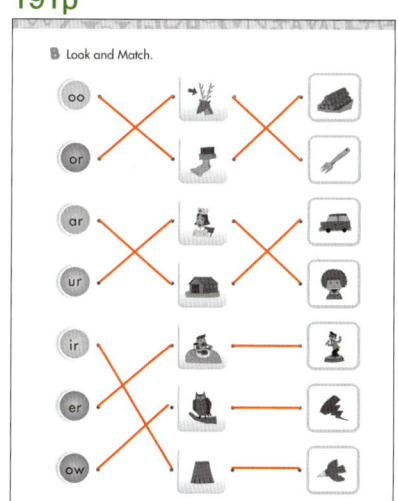

oo / or / ar / ur / ir / er / ow

192p

C Choose and Write correct letters.

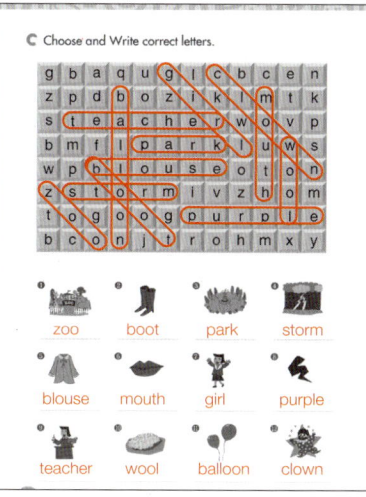

zoo / boot / park / storm
blouse / mouth / girl / purple
teacher / wool / balloon / clown

193p

D Check the right letters.

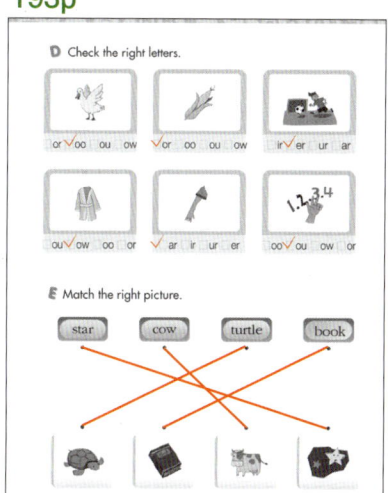

E Match the right picture.

star / cow / turtle / book

Answer Key

194p

F Write the missing letters.

m<u>oon</u> b<u>rown</u> b<u>ird</u> s<u>inger</u>

f<u>ork</u> s<u>occer</u> g<u>oose</u> c<u>loud</u>

n<u>urse</u> a<u>rm</u> s<u>hort</u> c<u>ook</u>

o<u>wl</u> d<u>inner</u> c<u>orn</u> l<u>ook</u>

195p

Final Test

A Check the correct picture.

au aw

or ar

ee ea

ou ow

196p

B Write the missing letters.

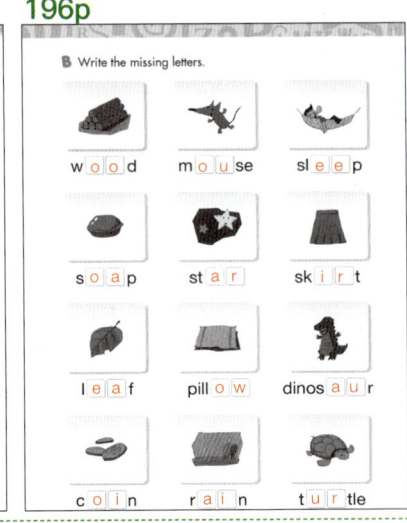

w o o d   m o u se   sl e e p

s o a p   st a r   sk i r t

l e a f   pill o w   dinos a u r

c o i n   r a i n   t u r tle

197p

C Circle the correct pictures.

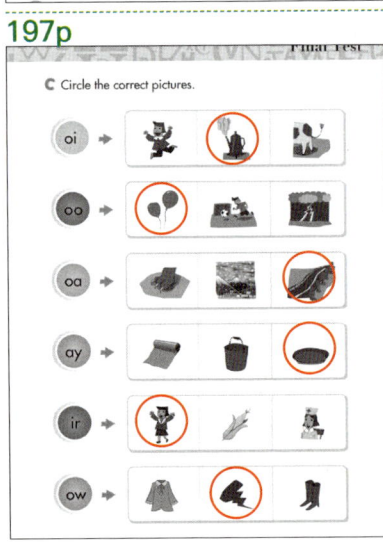

oi

oo

oa

ay

ir

ow

198p

D Choose and Write correct letters.

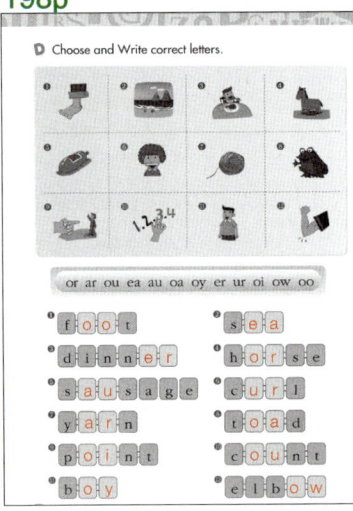

or ar ou ea au oa oy er ur oi ow oo

f o o t   s e a
d i n n e r   h o r se
s a u s a ge c u r l
y a r n   t o a d
p o i n t   c o u n t
b o y   e l b o w

199p

E Write the correct words.

book car shirt house

tea yellow mail join

toy pool horn cow

play straw eat gown

206 Workbook

어린이 파닉스 기술을 마스터
Jump Up Phonics + Workbook시리즈

총 4권으로 구성된 Phonics 시리즈
파닉스를 단어뿐만 아니라 스토리를 통해 익힘.
신나는 챈트와 다양한 액티비티로 반복
연습리뷰와 테스트 Unit은 재미있게 복습할 수 있도록 구성

책속 부록
재미있는 활동과 놀이를 통해 영어의 기초적인 내용을 학습

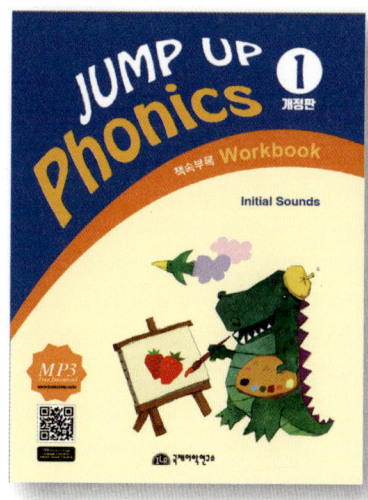

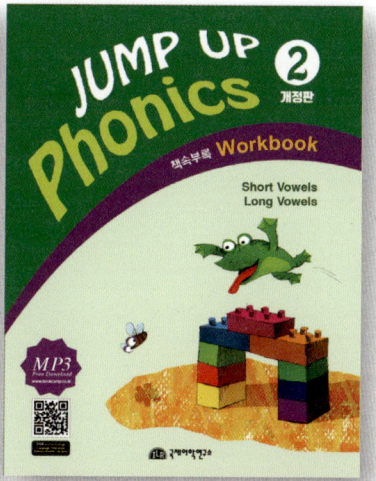

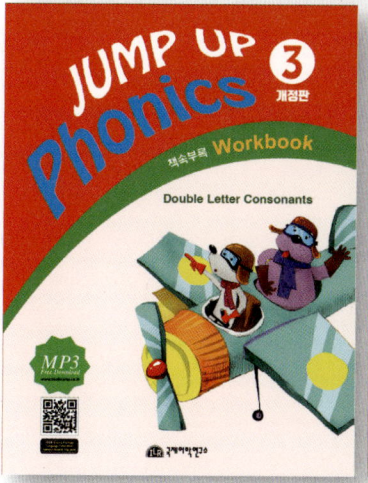

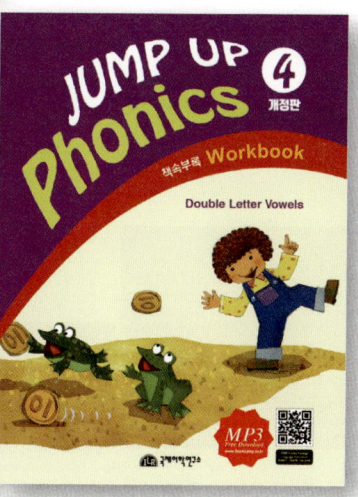